We introverts have great power. You may not believe it because of what you have been told, but it is true. Don't listen to those who say you are less; you are not. You were born with a quiet greatness. There is nobody on Earth quite like you, and nobody can take that away.

Leadership for Introverts

Path of Life Assessment graphic designed by graphicsden on fiverr.com.

Port Bell, Inc.
2602 S 38th St #361
Tacoma WA 98409
www.portbell.com

ISBN: 978-0-692-96872-7

First edition: May 2018

Leadership For Introverts

www.leadershipintroverts.com

By Dr. Ty Belknap

Leadership for Introverts

Chapter 1 ~ Introverts Make Great Leaders

A certain young man, born in the back woods of Kentucky, had a difficult childhood. He loved books and loved reading. But his father, a difficult man, thought books were a waste of time. He discouraged the boy from reading to the point that he would sometimes burn the few books the boy acquired.

The boy grew up during a tough time, and sometimes had to work to help keep his family from starving. The boy's father saw no good reason to read, so the boy would hide his books and read in the middle of the night after working 12-14 hour days.

He didn't have much to talk about other than the stories he read, but his neighbors loved hearing about them; so he ended up being a bit of a storyteller in his neighborhood.

It's interesting to see how this introvert was coaxed out of his shell. To go from a child who read against his father's wishes to being a neighborhood speaker is fascinating. But his story didn't stop there.

The man and his father did not get along well at all, so he vowed to leave as soon as he could. But the family moved to Illinois and he felt responsible for them so stayed with his brothers and sisters for a while longer.

He finally got out on his own at age 21, but he was still extremely poor, so he read whatever he could get his hands on. This usually meant that he read political flyers and articles from magazines and newspapers other people left behind.

The more he learned about politics, the more he talked about it to those around him. Combined with his ability to tell stories, this introvert soon found himself being a public speaker. From there, he got into politics.

Of course, it didn't happen the next day, week, or year. But eventually Abraham Lincoln became the 16th President of the United States.

\ \ \

Introverts can make great leaders; but quite often we have leadership thrust upon us, it is not something we look for. This statement, like many in this book, is a generality and does not fit for everyone. However, most introverts are happy to live outside the limelight.

It is time, however, to take our rightful place in the world, so…

Introverts Unite! Let's get together in a big group and talk about the weather. Oh, wait, that's a motto for extroverts. How about...

Introverts Divide! Let's all find quiet places where we can shed the anxieties of a busy day and concentrate on the task at hand.

Introverts and extroverts are very unique personality types, and the way each type thinks is vastly different. If you are reading this book, you either consider yourself an introvert, or you want to understand introverts more. Either way, you are at the right place.

Many introverts are happy with the way they are. And if you're not, that's your problem - Matthew Hutson

This world is full of loud sports events, loud parties and loud traffic. It's full of open office layouts, big gathering holiday events, and more meetings than you can shake a stick at (is there more of anything than you can shake a stick at?).

Group brainstorming, in-person networking, and social networks are the norm. This is an extroverted world, or so the extroverts would have us believe.

But, according to recent studies by Meyers-Briggs and in scientific magazines[1], *over half* the people in the world are introverts.

> *For Extroverts: Can you spot the introvert? Introverts, raise your hands (yeah, right!). Extroverts would be surprised at how many people are introverts because we have learned to act at being extroverts. Extroversion is expected in the United States, as it is expected in most of the western world.*

Just about any team that gets formed will have introverts and extroverts, but which type is the better fit to be a team leader? Extroverts are quite often chosen to lead because they are the ones to speak up first. And introverts, by nature, are willing to let someone else lead even when they have more knowledge and skills because it will mean that they don't have to stand in front of a group and talk.

But, the job of the leader is not just to talk and push the group forward. It is also the role of the leader to listen and adjust the plan based on other people's input and ideas. Yes, extroverts can do that, but introverts were born to do it.

Introverts, Extroverts, and Ambiverts, Oh My!

It might be good to better define an introvert versus an extrovert before I get too far in the leadership aspects of this book. Note: These are general differences. There are some extroverts that will identify with these traits and some introverts may not.

Or you might be an Ambivert; meaning you may show traits of extroversion or introversion at different times.

Consider this: It's a holiday weekend. You have three days off to do whatever you want. On top of that, you got a bonus recently so you have some extra money as well. Which situation sounds more enticing to you?

1. Find the hottest party in town and book a table for the entire weekend. Send out an evite over social media to everyone you know (and a few people you don't know), and get ready to talk the night away with friends. If you're lucky, you will meet a few new people as well.
2. Find a nice getaway place, somewhere to go for the weekend away from the crowds. Gather a stack of movies and books, or just enjoy nature alone or with a few close friends.

There have been many studies that have tried to help people understand whether they are an extrovert or introvert, and of course when personalities are involved nothing is perfect. But the simplest way I have come up with is how you recharge.

Think about the two points above. Which one charges you up, and which one drains you? In general, extroverts recharge by being around other people. They like social situations and feel energized by being in a group, the larger the better.

Being alone for long periods will drain an extrovert. Introverts recharge by being alone or in very small groups. They enjoy introspection and spending time thinking.

In social situations, you will generally find introverts engaged in a one on one conversation or in groups of three to five people. Larger groups tend to have a couple conversations going on at one time, but introverts have a difficult time switching from one conversation to another.

So, the larger the group dynamic, the more quickly an introvert's energy will drain from trying to keep up.

Introverts process during quiet times. They tend to think about answers and come to a conclusion before they begin to talk, which is why they do not do as well in larger social groups.

A social situation with a large group of people can seem daunting to an introvert, and it may make them feel uncomfortable and stressed. Of course, anyone under stress can have difficulty thinking; but an introvert's mind will seem like it is shutting down in such situations.

Replying to questions and keeping up with several conversations at one time can sometimes seem like a herculean task when introverts find themselves in large social groups.

Brainstorming in groups does not usually work for introverts; neither does working in cubicles where people can easily lean over and interrupt work. In fact, some recent studies[2] show that the new type of open office model is actually a deterrent to creativity even for extroverts.

For Extroverts: The late bloomer.
Ever have a brainstorming session and then, a day or two after the session is over, someone emails you with a suggestion as good as any produced during the session? That person is probably an introvert.

Some may think that introverts are wall-flowers, party poopers, or maybe even boring people. And America is known as an extroverted country; it is the land of Capitalism and the home of the salesman.

But, some of the richest and most influential Americans are self-described introverts. Abraham Lincoln, Bill Gates, Barak Obama, and Rosa Parks[3] are just a few of many American introverts.

Introverts Can Be Leaders?

Leadership is a lifetime of lessons - J. Robert Clinton[4]

Introverts are just as, if not more, capable of leading a team toward goals as extroverts are; they just go about it in a different way. It is time for introverts to rise up, embrace their nature, and understand that the deafening silence which extroverts hate is like a warm fire on a cool winter's evening to us. We have everything it takes to be great leaders, and we have natural leadership skills that some extroverts have trouble learning. We just need to understand and accept ourselves for who we are (maybe we are super heroes in disguise).

Super Heroes

Companies make money by giving people what they want. Since introverts are more likely to be found reading books and watching movies, is it any wonder that most super heroes are portrayed as introverts?

Think of the hero or heroine of most fantasy and science fiction books. They are almost always quiet, unassuming, and reluctant to be the hero. They are underdogs, people that seem to be more comfortable burying their face in a book than saving the world. Basically, introverts (one exception being the guy in red iron).

Just look at the guy in the red cape. He poses as a photographer at a newspaper when he is not saving the world, socially awkward and an introvert.

The billionaire super hero in the black cape is virtually a loner. The only time he goes out in public is to throw the authorities off. His best friend is his butler, which would fit for an introvert. Introverts have fewer friends than extroverts, but they have deep relationships with their friends.

Introverts Are Better Designed To Be Leaders

Extroverts make friends easily and are, by nature, more boisterous than introverts so they are easier to spot. It is easier to listen to an extrovert because they are more comfortable in casual conversations.

It also seems that some introverts think they need to act like extroverts in order to fit in (I know that is how I felt when I was younger). Everything just *seems* to be easier for extroverts, but that is not necessarily true.

The Chemicals in Our Brain

When it comes to gratification, there are four basic chemicals (neuro-transmitters) in our brain that govern the good sensations that we feel: Endorphins, serotonin, dopamine, and oxytocin. This is not a brain chemistry lesson... well, maybe a bit, but it won't be deep.

Endorphins are, for lack of a better word, a selfish neuro-transmitter chemical. Think of Endorphins as a natural form of morphine[5] (although about 4x more powerful than morphine). They are the chemicals that get released when we work out, run hard, ride for endurance, or do any activity that requires a lot of physical exertion.

When a person exerts him/herself beyond what is normal for them, it damages the muscles. And, naturally, when a part of the body gets damaged the brain registers it as pain. Endorphins mask a certain level of pain.

Have you ever had a time where you were doing something physical, like cleaning the garage, and noticed that you cut your finger or hand because you saw the blood? Then, shortly after you noticed that blood, you started to feel pain?

Endorphins were masking the pain before you saw the blood. But, once you did see it, you told your brain that where there is blood, there should be pain. And your brain listened to you and let you feel the pain by reigning in the endorphins.

Serotonin is a needy neuro-transmitter. It is a chemical that is released when a person feels liked, wanted or needed. And yes, I do mean "needy" in a good way. Without serotonin, people would not want to be leaders because this feel-good neuro-transmitter is released when leaders do a good job and those under him show appreciation.

Extroverts seem to have the need to produce this chemical more than introverts do.[6] One may assume, on the surface, that this is a good quality for a leader, but the *need* to produce this neuro-transmitter can backfire. A leader may make a decision that the people like, but is not in their best interest, in order to get a serotonin kick.

Introverts do not have as much of a need to produce more serotonin than is already floating around in their brain, which is why introverts do not crave the admiration of others as much as extroverts. It can also help introverts look at a situation and make a decision more on its merits than on the need to please others.

Dopamine is the domain of the extrovert, and it could be the number one reason why extroverts don't make as good of leaders as they want us to think. The second of the "needy" neuro-transmitters, dopamine is released when a person accomplishes something.

". . . In the business world today we receive a burst of dopamine with each marker we hit on our way toward the end goal." Simon Sinek, *Leaders Eat Last*

Winning a race, coming in first, making sales quotas, achieving a goal, or even attaining a step closer to a goal all release dopamine into our systems. This happens with extroverts and introverts, but extroverts *crave* this release more than introverts do.

Dopamine doesn't care about laying off employees as long as the manager gets a pat on the back for the numbers looking good. Dopamine also doesn't care about tripping an opponent as long as you are number 1 at the end of the event. Extroverts strive to be number 1 more than introverts. But, a leader is not number 1, his team is.

God created us with the need to help others. This is not a normal reaction in the animal kingdom. Gazelles will allow lions and tigers to eat the weak so the strong will survive. But humans were made to protect the weak and fragile. And God put a drug into our brain to reward us for this.

Oxytocin is the leadership neuro-transmitter of the brain. It is the drug that gets released when we help someone else and is our body's way of rewarding good leadership. Both extroverts and introverts crave oxytocin, and the more a person does for others, the more that person wants to do for others, the more oxytocin is released.

In fact, some recent studies have shown that more oxytocin gets released when we help someone that has no way of helping us back. Oxytocin is also being credited with helping to reduce depression. It is difficult to feel depressed when you are helping others.

So much has been learned about neuro-transmitters in the brain the last 40 years (think of this; the word "endorphin" was first defined in 1971). But these are not the only reasons introverts can make great leaders.

Introverts Have Natural Leadership Qualities

Researchers Jalili and Mall-Amiri recently conducted a study about whether extrovert or introvert teachers were better at classroom management. The researchers concluded that extroverts were, by far, better classroom managers of adult learners. However, the criteria for the study were things like "interactive discussion, group project, and experiential learning." [7]

Those are all *extroverted activities.* Of course extroverted teachers would be better at managing those tasks, but they would only be better at managing *half* of the class. The introverts in the class would pretend to be a willing part of it because they are the students and want a good grade. However, the entire study is skewed toward extroverted behavior.

A better class manager, or leader, would take a more ambivert approach and design a curriculum that switches between extroverted and introverted tasks. But extroverts are more likely to "fly by the seat of their pants" and do whatever comes to mind in the moment. And, since an extrovert is thinking it up, it would be an extroverted activity. Introverts are more likely to take time to think about how to best manage a diverse team than extroverts would.

There are some activities that generally come more naturally to introverts. Keep in mind that some extroverts will do these tasks well, and some introverts would rather be in a large group than do these items. These are just things that introverts generally do better, such as:

- Listening is an activity that introverts do well. Introverts like deep conversations, either one-to-one or in a small group.

Because of this, introverts need to be able to listen. They have the ability to listen to what is being said and what is not being said so they can learn a person's meaning behind the words.

- Writing is an individual task. It is difficult to write in a group because you need to internalize what you are thinking and then get it down to words. And it is difficult to accomplish that when a lot of people are talking at the same time.
- Critical thinking: This is a tough one. I know extroverts that are good at critical thinking, but the very nature of introverts makes this much easier than it would be for extroverts. However, introverts are not known to be critical thinkers in general because they rarely speak out. And since introverts can shut down in group settings, activities like brainstorming sessions do not work for introverts.

Don't get me wrong, I have nothing against extroverts. It takes both introverts and extroverts to make the world go around. And, I personally believe that an introvert/extrovert marriage is the best way to go. Yes, there are more difficulties. But, if the two of you work together to see the strengths each of you brings to the table, there is nothing you will not be able to do. Plus, it is an advantage for an extrovert to have an introvert partner since introverts are smarter than extroverts.

"A 2012 study completed by Randy Buckner of Harvard University discovered that . . . extroverts had less gray matter."[8] So, there we have it, proof that extroverts are less intelligent than introverts. And no, it's not true; I butchered that quote.

This study showed that extroverts had less gray matter specifically in the prefrontal cortex of the brain; while they had more gray matter than introverts in other areas of the brain. The scientists hypothesized that this could be an indicator of introvert or extrovert tendencies. However, it had no bearing on intelligence.

But it does make one stop and ponder. If our brains are hard-wired to be more inner-focused than extroverts, and we make up half the population, then half the people we lead are also introverts.

What About Ambiverts?

Introversion and extroversion are not absolutes. There are people that are the life of the party; but they recharge by being alone. And there are people that are wall-flowers but recharge by being around other people.

Very few people are pure introverts (hermits are a good example) and very few people are pure extroverts (the socialite everyone knows is a good example). Most people are in between the two extremes and some fall right in the middle.

Ambiverts are a low percentage of people that equally show extroversion and introversion. An Ambivert can read a book for hours on end or enjoy a party for hours on end without feeling anxious and needing a break. Simply put, Ambiverts enjoy all the positive traits, and can suffer all the negative traits, of both extrovert and introvert personalities.

Chapter 2 ~ The Internal You

Misfit in Your Own Land

Brett is a guy in his twenties. He has a decent job that he likes, but he doesn't seem to be getting ahead as fast as he expected. He works hard, but his boss doesn't recognize his contributions.

Brett has a few friends that he hangs out with after work, but not many. He is not big on sports, even though he often watches it with his friends. He would rather watch a television show or go on a hike.

His dating life is almost non-existent. He doesn't like the loud, chaotic scene of nightclubs, but doesn't know where else to go. He has tried online dating sites, but the pressure of meeting in person is almost as bad as going up to a woman in a nightclub.

Brett doesn't understand why he is so different from his friends. They are outgoing and easy to talk to. They make new friends easily and have active dating lives. Brett is an introvert. But, all his friends are extroverts, and when he does go out with them, they do extroverted activities. Brett needs to move to a new city.

\ \ \

Are You Living In The Wrong City?[1]

Imagine a land where there are three cities: Social City, Iland, and Weeville. Social City is a place where socializing in groups is the norm and having alone time is frowned upon. Socialcitians talk... a lot. They talk over each other, happily switching from topic to topic and carrying on conversations with two or three people at a time.

They will even talk to one or two people in person while talking on the phone at the same time. Socialcitians are boisterous, and they enjoy talking about their accomplishments.

Every person in Social City lives in one building and there is a huge courtyard in the middle of the building where everyone gathers night and day. Team sports are being played in different areas and the fans are very vocal in cheering them on.

There is a constant murmur of conversation in Social City no matter when you might be up. Families (and singles) have their own places to live, but there are signs on the doors saying "please do not knock. Come on in." The word stranger does not exist in Social City.

Iland is close to Social City, but it is a vastly different place. Iland is a city with a lot of pathways and trees. You have to look close to see the houses because they are all hidden behind shrubbery and gated fences. But there are many houses. In fact, each family (or single person) has their own house.

There are no large buildings anywhere. Even the stores are small, spread out all around Iland so there is always one close by. However, Ilanders prefer to order from the store over the internet with packages delivered to their door. This alleviates the dreaded possible conversation while waiting in the checkout line.

Iland is quiet. Few conversations can be heard, and those that are heard are neither loud nor involve many people. There are very few phone conversations. Ilanders usually either text or email others when needed. Immediate responses to texts and emails are frowned upon. Ilanders expect others to take their time when writing back.

Restaurants are designed in a way that there are only booths with high-backed seats so patrons do not have to see neighbors. This allows for uninterrupted book reading or quiet conversations during meals.

There are sports in Iland; but they are either individual sports like hiking and rock climbing, or they are small team sports like beach volleyball and tennis.

Conversation areas are placed all around the city of Iland but they are small, accommodating 3-5 people at the most. You will rarely see a large gathering in Iland.

Small talk is frowned upon there. Talking, when required, should be on topic using as few words as possible.

In between Social City and Iland is the town of Weeville. Weeville is where Ilanders and Socialcitians get together to work and interact. There are a few people that live in Weeville, but not many. Most of the people you will find in Weeville after work hours are Socialcitians getting together for an after work party or social gathering (and, of course, the after party will be back in Social City). Ilanders occasionally join the party, but they do not stay long; the comfort of their quiet home calls to them within an hour or two.

Socialcitians talk fast and loud. Ilanders are quiet and think before speaking. This usually means that Socialcitians get their way since by the time an Ilander is ready to speak, a decision has often already been made. Because of this, much of Weeville is designed for Socialcitians.

Most office spaces have been created using cubicles or an open office design. This allows Socialcitians to happily talk across the office at each other. According to them, it also helps with brainstorming.

However, some studious Ilanders have concluded that the more open an office design, the less work gets done. They have found that even Socialcitians need a quiet space in order to do their best work.

But, regardless of that, the open office designs are stifling the Ilanders creativity and productivity. They do not understand why the Socialcitians continue to go in a direction that is not working. But the Ilanders are having a difficult time trying to figure out how to tell this to the Socialcitians.

Ilanders are starting to realize that the reason they are not heard may not be because they are shy; and it might not be because they are timid. The reason they are not heard is simply because Socialcitians do not understand them.

And such is the current state of the three cities.

Alone, Not Lonely

"I worry about you being alone all the time," is a saying many introverts have heard from well-meaning friends that don't understand. Being alone, to an introvert, is a time of relaxing solitude. It does not mean we are lonely.

Extroverts, on a Friday night, might be thinking of who they are going to call to go listen to a local band with. Or maybe there's a special social event their networking group is hosting. Dancing is always an option. But maybe they just want to get together with a bunch of friends at the local pub, eat some food and hang out.

And they make you feel like there's something wrong with you because you don't want to do any of those things. What extroverts don't realize is that you have been social 9-5 all week long without a break.

Friday night is for finding a comfortable blanket to wrap up in next to a fire with a good book or a movie. You might like a quiet dinner with the family or a few friends, but definitely not "hanging out," which is cool-speak for talking without a purpose.

Believe in Yourself

You have a quiet power residing in you, and that power can make for a great leader. However, as an introvert, much of your life was probably spent hearing things like "why are you so shy," "what's wrong with you," "why aren't you happy," and more.

The fact is that we don't have to have a stupid smile on our faces to be happy. There is nothing wrong with us. And, although it is more likely for an introvert to be shy than an extrovert (even though there are some shy extroverts), not all introverts are shy. We have just been told that we are shy for so long that we have started believing it.

> *For Extroverts:*
> *Introverts are cautious and sometimes skittish, especially around new people. Hear them out when they talk. If you put them down, talk over them or ignore them when they do finally speak; chances are they won't make that mistake again.*

Being quiet isn't being shy. But introverts have several hurdles to jump over. There are a lot of limiting beliefs ("why are you so different?") that need to be shattered so we can unleash our amazing potential. We are not different; half the populations of the world are introverts. We are strong. Many of us just don't realize how strong we are because those limiting beliefs are holding us back.

I had some severe limiting beliefs when I was younger, and it took decades to shatter them. I did it mostly on my own, but also with some help from people who mistakenly gave me advice (meaning, they were not intentionally trying to give me advice, but I took what they said to heart). It was difficult to find people for me to go to for help, partly because I didn't realize what I needed help with.

But now I do. An introvert's power is like the sound of ocean waves hitting rocks on a windy day. It doesn't seem like much, but it would take a great deal of work to stop the waves from hitting the rocks.

However, most introverts don't realize that they have this power. They are "quiet" and "shy," just like they have been told all their lives, so they do not speak up. But it's not because they are shy, it's because they need help in understanding the power they possess.

I sat at a park bench one lazy summer afternoon, enjoying the sun and watching my children play. Not far from me was a woman I assumed was an introvert from the way she acted. She looked up from her book and called her daughter over. This introverted woman told her daughter to play with the other children more, because socializing was important. Here was an introverted mother telling her introverted daughter to be more extroverted. I realized that day how much we have allowed society to bend us to the will of extroverts.

We need people we can trust to go to, and family is not always the best option. They may think they are giving you advice, but they may actually just be telling you how they would lead your life. Sometimes, the people around us with the best intentions are the ones that give the worst advice.

"If I were you," and "what you should do" are two sayings that make me cringe, and I heard them a lot. The best advice I ever got was from people that mostly asked me questions; they were people that were using coaching techniques, but didn't realize they were coaching.

Now, with coaching being a buzzword (there are no longer toilet cleaners, they are sanitation coaches), it is difficult to find the right person to talk to. It seems everyone and their brother wants to be a life coach. So, if you decide to hire a life coach to help you, make sure they are professionally certified or have college credentials. You do not need to look for an introvert life coach either; it will not matter as long as the person is good at what they do.

So, are limiting beliefs stopping you? And if you change your beliefs, what would be possible? One of my favorite questions to ask is: "If there were nothing to stop you, what would you do?"

> *How is your Path of Life? What areas of your life are doing well, and what areas need to be improved? Take my exclusive Path of Life Assessment in Appendix 5 to see if your path is smooth or full of ruts.*

However you go about it, you must believe in yourself before others can believe in you. The path to leadership starts inside you.

Plan to Fail

There is only one way to fail: Give up. As long as you do not give up, you will not fail. There are not failures, only opportunities to learn. We learn more from overcoming obstacles than we do being a couch potato.

When was the last time you made a great discovery when everything was going smooth in your life? We tend to go with the flow during good times, wanting to ride it out as long as we can.

Sometimes we forget that life is like a mountain range; there are always going to be peak highs and valley lows. But it is in the valleys, the low points, when we make the most of opportunities that are around us.

The only way to truly fail is to not try. So why not plan to fail? A certain lady I know is a cold-calling salesperson. Personally, I think that is the most thankless job around, and I do not envy people who do that.

She knows that 19 out of 20 people will hang up on her (hopefully without using foul language before they do). Her goal is to get those 19 people out of the way quickly so she can talk to that one person who is really interested in what she is selling.

The other 19 people that hang up are not failures. She would not have the one person who wants to buy without them. So, plan to fail. If you are trying to get a business loan, plan on the first 10 banks saying no. It might even be worth it to go to the banks that you know will say no first so you can get them out of the way.

This would be difficult for an introvert, we do not handle rejection well (truth is, extroverts don't either). That is why it is important to plan on the no's. That way, they are not rejections; they are part of the plan.

Failing at something is an event. Being a failure is a mindset. You are only a failure if you decide to be one.

If, as a leader, you want to pitch an idea to your boss, plan on him/her saying no. Think about all the reasons they would say no, and write down ways to overcome every rejection. If they still say no, ask if they have time to talk about why they said no. Ask the boss if there were parts of the pitch he/she liked, and find out if there would be a way to modify it. The worst they are going to do is keep saying no.

If you work for a boss that says no to everything, especially if they don't tell you why or help you find another way, it may be time to free up your future and find a place that will respect you more. Read chapter 4 on Planning for Success, it will help a great deal in this type of situation.

Yes, it is extremely difficult to force yourself to go to your boss, in person, and pitch an idea. Every step of that activity has the potential of shutting you down. Then, to add on to it, you have to *plan* on the boss saying no? Is that like knowing it won't work before it even starts? Why even bring the idea to him/her if you are planning to fail? You don't want to get rejected yet again, do you? STOP

This is taking planning to fail a bit too far. And, as an introvert, I know we can create entire scenarios of the worst possible way a meeting can be acted out before it ever begins.

Turn your mind around and look at it from another perspective. You aren't really planning to fail, you are planning to overcome every opportunity to fail when you think of every "No" your boss might say and have an answer for it.

You will fail if you do not try. Babe Ruth was known around the world for having the most homeruns in baseball for many years (and some say he still holds that record). But Babe Ruth has another record. Do you know what it is?

Babe Ruth is one of the top leaders in strike outs. Was Babe Ruth a failure? He struck out 1330 times,[2] but he is thought of as one of the best players in the history of baseball. You can't get a home run if you don't swing at the ball. Yes, you may strike out sometimes; but every strikeout teaches you something.

Dr. Travis Bradbury summed up failing well in his article *10 Habits of Mentally Strong People*: "You have to make mistakes, look like an idiot, and try again."[3]

Chapter 3 ~ What/Who is a Leader?

Now that we better understand the general indications of an introvert, it is time to ask the question "what/who is a leader?" It is a good question, and the word has taken on a new meaning in the twenty-first century. Traditionally, a leader was thought of as one of two types of positions:

1. Anyone above a Private (or equivalent) in the military was traditionally considered a leader. Lieutenants, captains, and of course generals were considered leaders. Likewise, the President of the United States has commonly been called the Leader of the Free World.
2. People that volunteered to lead a ministry or a small group in a church setting were also traditionally considered leaders.

Now, anyone that used to be considered a manager, or anyone in authority over two or more people, is considered to be a leader. But, is there is a problem with distinguishing a leader in that way? In order to define a leader, a definition of leadership is in order.

John Maxwell describes leadership as "influence."[1] However, some think this is too broad. George Barna defines a leader as ". . . one who mobilizes; one who's focus is influencing people; a person who is goal driven; someone who has an orientation in common with those who rely upon him for leadership; and someone who has people willing to follow them."[2] My definition of leadership would be the willingness to show others the path by going down it first.

You may have noticed that none of these definitions specifically describes a leader as a person in a position of authority; a leader does not have to be a person in authority. The higher up the management ladder a person is, the more likely that person is a leader, but that is not always the case.

Corporations are full of managers with leaders below them. The manager will conduct a meeting and tell everyone what to do. Then, after the meeting, the employees will get with the leader, usually another employee, and discuss what they are really going to do.

So who is a leader? The answer is easy; everyone is a leader in one respect or another. If you ever, as a child, influenced your parents to buy a certain toy, you were exhibiting leadership skills. If any of your school friends followed you or took your advice, you were acting as a leader. And of course, if you are a parent, the question is moot: You are a leader.

Since everyone above the age of five is potentially a leader, the question you should ask yourself is not "how can I be a leader," but "how can I be a *good* leader?" Leaders come in more flavors than ice cream, and the news is full of leaders that took advantage over those that followed them. So what does it take to be a good leader?

A Bad Leader or a Good Leader?

If, as Maxwell says, leadership is influence, then every company that purports to be working in the best interest of the people should be a company full of leaders. Enron was a ". . . energy giant with $101 Billion in annual revenue that decided to cook the books in hopes of keeping shareholders happy."[3]

"In March 2001, just nine months before declaring bankruptcy, Enron signaled that it was having trouble."[4] Despite the indication that Enron was about to fall, between March and December 2001 nine of the top stock brokerages; including Merrill Lynch, J.P. Morgan, Bank of America, and Prudential, to name a few, told their investors to either hold onto their stock or to buy more stock in Enron.[5] They did that, even when they knew Enron was falling, because those companies owned a majority of Enron's shares.

The immorality of a select few caused widespread financial issues throughout the United States. In a Los Angeles Times article on the Enron bankruptcy (January 20, 2002), James Flannigan reported that the backlash was causing a wide spread political, legal, and investor crisis even a year later. This is a good example of bad leadership. It brought down a large organization and assisted in the recession of an entire country.

Glen Rowe, in his study, posited that: ". . . to achieve excellence in any organization it is necessary, ceteris paribus, to have ethical leaders in the most senior leadership positions, and that ethical leaders are needed to insure the long-term viability of organizations."[6]

Names like Warren Buffet, Mother Theresa, Mahatma Gandhi, and John Maxwell are famous for what the respective persons did; but, they are also famous for what they did not do. As far as I know, there has yet to be any substantiated evidence to their ever using their leadership influence for purely selfish pursuits.

The norm is to hear of a famous person or a leader who has used his/her influence for selfish means (Bill Clinton, Bill Cosby, Steve Wynn, Tammy Faye Bakker, etcetera.).

Neither is the church an asylum against corruption, nor has it ever been.

"Jim Bakker's 1989 conviction on twenty-four counts of broadcast fraud, mail fraud, and conspiracy was viewed widely as the death blow to similar evangelical TV empires in the United States; particularly as Bakker's fellow televangelists Jimmy Swaggart, Pat Robertson, and Jerry Falwell were eventually drawn into the controversies surrounding the control and bankruptcy of Bakker's Christian theme park, Heritage USA.

A national audience was treated over a period of months to revelations of adultery, hypocrisy, greed, hush money, and internecine maneuvering among these ministers of the gospel almost worthy of Claudian Rome."[7]

Everything is different, but nothing changes. We are in a technological age that is unprecedented in the history of the world. But pride, selfishness, selflessness, honesty, hate, and love are still as fresh in our hearts as they were thousands of years ago. We don't think of it this way, but most of those emotions are choices we make. We have no power over many things that happen to us, but all the power in deciding how to respond.

Linda Rule was a 16 year old girl that fell victim to a serial killer. During the trial, the families of the victims were allowed to give speeches to the accused. Every speech was full of hate and a hope for retribution about the killer.

That is why a manager may be able to force a person to produce; but a leader will help a person to understand why they want to produce. A manager may try to keep his workers down so he will have job security (If I don't teach anyone else to do my job, they can't fire me). But a leader will teach others to take his or her place, knowing that they will all rise up together.

Being

There are traits that make a good leader. Some (but by no means all) of those traits are: Humility, character, competence and intelligence. Each of these traits can be learned.

Humility

Just because an introvert is quiet, it does not mean that person is humble. Introverts are, in fact, sometimes accused of being arrogant. This usually stems from people that have not taken the time to understand introverts. It sounds quite arrogant of me to say that, doesn't it? However, introverts have been misunderstood. That is part of the reason why so many books about introverts have been published in recent years.

Introverts are seen as arrogant for one main reason: We don't talk much unless we know what we are talking about. For instance, I consider myself a computer nerd. I worked as a network engineer for government agencies and corporations such as Compaq and Microsoft for about 20 years. I know a lot about computers (I am one of the only parents I know whose children come to me for computer help).

I remember a party I attended where I talked the night away with two other people, about computers. The next day a friend called me and commented that he had never heard me talk so much. He was open with me, and mentioned that another person at the party thought I was being a bit arrogant. And he did not know what to say because he didn't realize how much I knew about computers. Although we had been friends for some time, he wasn't a computer person so I didn't talk to him much about that subject.

That is common among introverts. We have the ability to compartmentalize our lives, but that can sometimes confuse our friends. An introvert could tell a friend that they work in the HR department of a large corporation. But if that friend doesn't know much about human resources, the introvert may not go into detail about their job. So the next time the introvert meets up with another person that works in HR, they may have a long and detailed conversation that blows the introvert's friend away.

This is one glaring difference between introverts and extroverts. An extrovert may go on and on, talking about several different subjects. They may flit between the weather, their job, the latest viral social media post and their current health in a short period of time.

It's kind of like going to a carnival or a fair. There are many things to do, many rides to choose from, and each ride only takes a few minutes. An extrovert is good at talking about many different subjects, but they don't usually get very deep. Extroverts generally like to have conversations that are closer to the surface.

However, switching subjects too quickly will confuse an introvert. They prefer to stick to one subject and explore it like an adventurer who just found a cave and is excited to probe the entire depth of it. So when an introvert finds an audience for a subject they know well, they could go on and on and on, and get into great detail. An introvert could be seen as being arrogant in this instance if the recipient does not know them well or rarely hears them talk much.

However, humility does not mean staying quiet. A person can be humble while they talk about their accomplishments; and he or she can be humble while they talk about their work or a promotion. Being humble does not mean being subservient. Dictionary.com defines humble as being not proud or arrogant but being modest.

The introverted leader can show humility by talking about the accomplishments the team made rather than the accomplishments of the leader themselves. Humility is a combination of the leader taking the blame themselves and assigning praise to the team.

Character

Your character is who you are when nobody is watching. Do you act nice around other people and then go into a room by yourself and start yelling and screaming? Do you put on a face in public and then talk about people behind their back in private?

These are character flaws. And, like the other traits, there are ways to fix character flaws. Your flaws may be different than these, but you have character flaws. I know you don't want to hear that, but it is true.

I used to be more concerned with my own success than that of anybody else; and I have done things to get ahead in the past that I am not proud of. Although I still find myself thinking selfishly at times, that character flaw is nowhere near as large as it used to be. However, I still have to work on it as well as other character flaws.

Everybody has character flaws. Some people have small, little flea flaws and some people have flaws the size of a blue whale. And, chances are, each person has more than one flaw.

Sometimes we don't see our flaws. Or you might not see one flaw until another flaw has been worked on. I think of flaws like onions. You may have layers of flaws to work on, but each layer could be smaller than the last one.

Accepting that you have character flaws is a part of being a leader. Once you identify the flaws you have, you can begin to work on them. And as you work on your own flaws, you can help the members of your team work on theirs. However, the members of your team will not trust you to help them with their flaws if you are not open and honest about your own.

Competence

There is an activity that many positive motivational people have used to describe competence. The last person I heard it from was Zig Ziglar, but I don't think he was the first person to have said it. Here's the activity:

A baby knows nothing about tying shoes. The baby does not know what shoes are and does not know what shoelaces are. The baby is an unconscious incompetent.

The first time a child tries to tie his shoes; he fumbles around with the laces and does a terrible job. When he gets done, the laces are not actually tied. The child is a conscious incompetent because he knows that he needs to tie the laces but does not know how.

After much practice, the child ties the laces. The bow looks terrible, one loop is much larger than the other, and the knot is loose. But the laces are tied. The child is now a conscious competent. He knows that the laces need to be tied and he knows how to tie them.

Fast forward a period of time. The child jumps out of bed, grabs his shoes, ties them without even thinking about it, and runs out to start his day. The child is now an unconscious competent.

Competence is one of the easiest traits on this list that can be taught. In fact, everything else on this list goes through the competence activity above. We don't usually think about competence as we go through our daily lives; all we think about is that we have something new to learn and we need to learn it.

Luckily, introverts are often better at learning competence than extroverts. Unlike the generalization that men don't read instructions, many introverts do. That generalization is about extroverts who believe that doing equals progress, even if they don't know what it is they're doing. Or, to put it more simply, the "alpha male" stereotype.

Intelligence

Intelligence is on the list of top qualities in many leadership books, and intelligence can be learned. All you need to gain intelligence, or knowledge, is to read quality material.

It is knowledge that influences and equalizes the social condition of man; that gives to all, however different their political position, passions which are in common, and enjoyments which are universal. - Benjamin Disraeli

But intelligence without wisdom is a blowhard. Wisdom is intelligence put to action. I have had extremely intelligent professors that didn't have the wisdom of a puppy. One professor would happily lecture to the class for four days straight, but he would be using such technical speech that few people understood what he was saying.

He treated beginning classes like they were advanced students, and their grades reflected it. Some believed he treated them this way on purpose, putting them down for not understanding him better.

What was puzzling was that, on a one to one basis, this professor was kind and attentive. He would spend a great deal of time helping a student to understand the curriculum. He was almost two different people; one person a lecturer and the other a real person. He just didn't have the wisdom to see that he could be both.

Another professor did not talk like an academic at all. He even used street talk sometimes. He occasionally lectured the students, but just as often had open discussions during class.

This man was an extrovert to be sure. He would put the students into groups (ew), but would put students together based on their strengths and weaknesses to create a dynamic group. He showed tremendous wisdom in providing leadership even if he didn't understand how to work with introverts.

Doing

There are also specific things leaders do. A short list would be: Teaching others (or mentoring), vision casting, motivating and thinking. Some would argue that organization is in the list, and it does have its place, but many organizational tasks can be delegated.

Teaching Others

Lee Iacocca was considered to be a good leader. In the 1980s, he turned around the struggling Chrysler Corporation and started them down the track of being one of the biggest American automobile manufacturers again.

He convinced the American government to give Chrysler a loan before it was common to do so, and paid the loan back several years before the note was due. However, when he left, Chrysler again started going downhill; and the company continued in that direction for many years.

Every leader has weaknesses. The best leaders lead through their weaknesses; the leaders that are not as good will ignore their weaknesses and try to hide them. It is my opinion that teaching others was a weakness of Iacocca. The path that the Chrysler team took may have been very different if Iacocca would have personally trained one or more people to take the lead when he left.

Some people think that teaching others is very difficult, and it can be a daunting task. But teaching is usually little more than showing other people what you do and how you do it. A person who is not a leader would not train leaders. Granted, there are times when academic teachers have not actually done the things that they teach. The best teachers, however, have a great deal of experience in doing what they are teaching.

Vision Casting

I get frustrated with books that talk about the same thing in several different areas, so I will not do so here. There is a section on Creating Your Strategic Vision in Chapter 4.

Motivating

As Zig Ziglar used to say, motivation is like bathing. You don't have to do it regularly, but it is recommended. A leader needs to be a positive motivating factor to the team, and to do so the leader needs motivation him/herself.

Don't be a leader that says something like "I'm at the top of my field; I have nobody to go to." That is vanity talking, and has no place in true leadership. True leadership is knowing that you are never too good. There will always be someone that can teach you, and sometimes that will be your own team.

Leaders do need motivation. Luckily, there are thousands of ways to get it. Motivational seminars are going on all over the country, and the internet has opened up a whole new way of getting almost anything. There are more motivational videos on the internet now than any one person would want to watch. A great leadership trick would be to find an appropriate motivational video for the team and have everyone watch it. This has two benefits: The team and the leader all get motivation; and the leader didn't have to spend time creating it him/herself.

Thinking

Thinking is under doing? As a matter of fact, yes, and it is one of the things at which introverts excel. An important part of the introverted leader's role is actively thinking about tasks, and documenting what you think about.

The most successful people in the world routinely come up with new ideas, but how many of those ideas are good? If you had to come up with 1,000 mediocre ideas in order to come up with one million dollar idea, would you do it? The task is coming up with the mediocre ideas first.

Try to come up with 5-10 new ideas every day. The first four or five may be easy and the last two may be very difficult. But the last ideas you come up with may be the best of the bunch.

I try to write down 10 ideas a day. And I am happy to say that this book was one of the ideas I had. Sometimes I overlap with previous days, but I try not to do that. However, I pay special attention when I see a pattern emerging of similar ideas over several days, and you should also. Your mind is telling you something and it may be time to start listening.

Always write your ideas down. You already know what's going to happen if you don't (hint: nothing). Keep an electronic tablet (or a notebook for those of you that remember paper) with you at all times so you don't lose those precious ideas.

The Leader's Circle

Many books talk about leaders getting the right people on their team; but that is not the circle I'm talking about. The Leader's Circle is The Circle of Protection you, as a leader, put around your team. It is the zone of protection that you provide, a safe zone of understanding and trust. This is a place where ideas can flow freely and (constructive) criticism can be voiced without fear of losing one's job.

You may have worked at, or visited, a caustic office in the past. It was a place where the air was so thick with stress and fear that it choked you. In places like that, the leadership of the company provides no Circles of Protection for their staff.

And, more than likely, there were no great ideas being produced in that company. Communication was lacking. Workers didn't trust management, and management didn't trust the workers.

A company with that kind of atmosphere is, at best, stagnant; at worst, going down fast. The only way to quickly change a company like that is to change management. It is possible to re-train managers, but the trust is at a negative state and will take time to rebuild. Bringing in new blood is more likely to put the trust level closer to zero (making the circle very small), but at least it won't be negative anymore.

Every leader's Circle starts out small. It is impossible for a new leader to have a huge Circle of Protection. A leader may step into the position of a previous leader that had a larger Circle of Protection, but that does not belong to the new leader. The circle will naturally shrink to fit the comfort level of the leader.

However, if you follow the being and doing areas above, the Circle of Protection that you create will grow. And, of course, if you were known as a leader in an organization somewhere else, your circle will start out much larger than that of a brand new leader with no experience.

Regardless of who the leader is, the leader's Circle of Protection has nothing to do with the bottom line. It does not care about sales figures or net profit. The leader's Circle of Protection only protects people.

Leaders care about people. Managers care about numbers. However, numbers don't make sales, people do. So creating an environment designed to help people succeed will raise numbers faster than creating a poisonous environment that puts people down for failing.

Unfortunately, this is the norm in today's society. Do an internet search on how many people like their jobs, and you will get article upon article about how 70-80% of people dislike or hate their jobs.

You can change that as a leader. You have the power to create a positive environment for those you lead even if you don't get support from above. Of course, you don't want to go against upper management; but all they may care about are the numbers. And, since happy employees generally produce better than employees that are not happy, the leader's Circle of Protection should have the natural bonus of the department or area doing better for the company or organization.

Creating your leader's Circle of Protection could make for both happier employees and happier management at the same time. Now, that is true leadership. And once you have the proper people in your circle, it's time to make them successful.

Chapter 4 ~ 6 Steps to Success Planning

Give me six hours to chop down a tree, and I will spend the first four sharpening my axe - Abraham Lincoln.

Success Planning is at the core of what leaders do. Leaders plan for success and then implement that plan.

This chapter is designed to be read through twice. You may already have an idea of a vision and mission, but I recommend a new way of designing them. So don't skip this.

Read through the chapter once; then the second time start at the end of the chapter, in the section called "The Getaway." It helps you break down success planning into bite-sized pieces. Just like looking up at a mountain; it seems intimidating at first, but all you have to do is take one step at a time.

The first step is the most difficult, but you have already taken that step. You are reading this book. Each step will be a bit easier from this point on.

I learned an interesting correlation of two statistics from the Economic Development department of the county in which I live (and this is true across the country): 85% of all small businesses fail in the first 12-18 months. And, 85% of all small businesses do not have a written business plan or plan of success; their why, core values, vision, mission, target market and strategy. That is not a coincidence.

The same is true of relationships. When you got into your relationship (or your last relationship if you are not now in one), did you ask why you wanted to be with that person? Or was the first thing that came to mind lust?

That's okay, physical attraction is important. But did you ask your potential partner what his/her core values were? How about her life mission? What was his strategic vision for his future? What was the strategy they had designed to get from where they are now to where they want to be?

Asking these questions is not romantic, but it is extremely practical. And the answers to these questions will help you determine how long your relationship will last. How do their answers compare to yours?

Are you in the right relationship? Are you working in the right job at this time? Where is your life headed? And why are you going down that road? If you are doing the same thing today because it is what you did yesterday, and you don't have a clear path to the future then you are heading toward a dead-end. So what needs to change?

In what area of your life do you need help? What area is suffering the most? This is the area that I call the low hanging fruit. Imagine walking down a path and you find an apple tree. You see big, juicy apples way at the top of the tree, but there are also big juicy apples right at eye level. You will not exert the energy to climb the tree to get the apples above when there is a scrumptious one right in front of you.

Look at your life issues in the same way; find the low hanging fruit. What is the issue that's right in front of your eyes? It's easy to see that there is a problem and finding a path to remove the problem may not be too difficult. It is also the area where small successes can be a big deal; and that will help bolster your self-confidence.

> *Introverts are not the only ones that can suffer from low self-confidence. Some extroverts have low self-confidence also; they just hide it better than we do.*

And keep in mind; the better you lead your own life, the more others will want follow you. So what is the area of your life that needs the most work, and why do you think that is so? If you are not sure, take the Path of Life Assessment in Appendix 5. But take care; you may be surprised at what you find.

Success planning in life begins with why, but it does not end there. In fact, no matter what area of your life you are working on, there are six basic planning steps that will help you be more successful. They are:

- Why: What is your sizzle?
- Core Values: What do you stand for?

- Mission: What are you doing?
- Vision: What will it look like when you get where you are going?
- Target market: Who will benefit from this?
- Strategy: What steps do you need to take to accomplish your vision?

These six steps answer six basic questions: Who, what, when, where, how and why. And I'm sure you recognize what these questions are: They are the basis for every compelling story ever written. Your why is the first step in writing the story of you.

Once you know your sizzle, your why, you will want to determine your core values. From there you can work on the rest of the planning steps (HINT: This may seem overwhelming at first, but I know you can do it. Each section has manageable steps so you can accomplish this. And the Getaway section shows how you can take two days to do it all. Think of it as a working vacation).

The first two steps, Why and Core Values, may seem to be the least important of the steps but they are actually the most important. Here is an example why:

I used to run a web design company. And, like most companies, the first couple of years were difficult. Money was sometimes scarce, and it seemed to swing between feast and famine. During a time when we were scrambling for new clients, I got an offer to do a web site that could net five figures. That was one of the largest accounts we could have landed at the time.

I'm sure many other people would have jumped at the opportunity. It would have opened the doors to be able to add several hundred thousand dollars a year to the bottom line of the business, but the site was morally questionable. I asked myself two questions:

1. Would I feel embarrassed to tell existing and possible new clients about that project (speaks to why)?
2. Does that project fit with my core values?

I would have been embarrassed to tell other clients about that project and it did not fit with my core values, so I declined the offer. I personally believe that something happens inside us when we say no to a short term benefit that may come back to bite us in the future. That kind of decision helps our self-confidence a great deal.

And, in case you are wondering, the web design company flourished. I ran the business for almost 15 years, and enjoyed every project I worked on. We said no to several questionable projects, and never looked back with regret.

So do not skip the Why and Core Values sections. The answers to those two questions will be the determining factor with every decision you make.

Success Begins With Why

(Watch the Success Begins with Why Webishop (webinar/workshop) at www.webishops.com under the Success Planning series)

Why do you do what you do? What motivates you? Is it money? Do you feel a need to please others? Or, do you do it because you don't know what else to do? I hope this section will change your mind if any of these is your current motivation. Determining why you do something will improve your chances of success, be it in:

- Relationships
- Career
- Business
- Life

Why are you doing what you are doing? Why do you want to do something new? What motivation is behind that? Get to the core of your why.

There is a man in the construction industry who builds beautiful houses; and he also does repair work on existing houses. The repair work does not make him nearly as much money as building a house, but he insists on taking those types of jobs. And, that insistence goes back to his why. He wants people to feel safe and comfortable in their homes. A family will not feel safe in a home that leaks or has cracks in the walls.

> *The book* Good to Great *by Jim Collins talks about getting the right people on the bus, but he assumes the "bus" is already there. Make sure you have built the right bus first. Your Why and your Vision are your bus.*

But why does he have a passion for that? Where is the core of that passion? It went back to when he was a child. His father was injured right before a storm hit the town where he lived. The roof was damaged, but his father could not get up to patch it.

In desperation, his mother got up on the roof and secured a tarp over the damaged area. He remembered being six years old, out in a huge rain storm, holding a wet, slick wooden ladder for his mother to get up and down on and feeling very scared for her. He ended up creating a business designed to help people with construction problems, and it has been very successful.

Why are you doing what you are doing? What is the reasoning behind it? Your story is your why. And it's a good thing to write it down, because you can't effectively tell other people your story unless you know exactly what it is (you do not have to tell anyone else your why, you can just write it down to solidify it for yourself). Take action.

However, you do not have to take action this minute. The Getaway section at the end of this chapter has strategies on how to take action for all of the success planning steps. So, for now, think about your why. Start to chew on what your passion really is for doing what you are doing.

When you think of why, is the first thing that comes to mind dollar signs? For many people it is, at least on the surface. But, when you drill down a bit, you may find that money has little to do with your Why. Money is just a means to an end; it can't do much. American money is a thin, flimsy cloth. You can't weave it into clothes, and it does not even burn well.

Don't get me wrong, money is important. It's kind of like gravity, we are usually glad it is there. And it is much more fun to have money than to not have money, that's for sure! But it also depends on what you are going to do with it. A drug abuser that gets more money probably isn't going to invest it wisely and it's almost certainly not going to make him happier.

So, if you see dollar signs as your Why, I encourage you to ask yourself; what's behind the money? What will the money give you? You might say that you want to be a millionaire. Why would you like to be a millionaire? So you can have a million dollars? What will those million dollars do for you?

Your why probably won't be money, it will be the resources you can get for the money. Maybe it will be a better house, a more secure lifestyle, retirement, vacations or something similar. Whatever that why is, you will probably find that money is in the middle of the why, not at the source. Because, if your only goal is the accumulation of money, then you will be the richest person in the cemetery and someone else will spend your money. So you may as well spend it yourself.

What is the driving passion behind what you are doing? What is your sizzle? If you do not have one, or if you are only working for a paycheck, I urge you to do one of two things:

1. Find a reason to be passionate about what you do; figure out what it might be. Maybe you are working so you can afford to send your children to college. But, do not make your why so you can retire. Do you really want to work 30+ years in a job you don't like? Do you want to continue down a career path that is boring and unfulfilling? What will that do to your joy? I believe that behind every grumpy old man/woman is a career lived for a

paycheck. Or a marriage lived for the children. It is not worth it. Find a passionate why.

2. Get out. I don't say this about marriage. I truly believe that, if two people work at their marriage on a consistent basis, they will never fall out of love with each other. But, it does take work. However, as far as your career or other endeavors, if you cannot find a passionate why, figure out what you can do that does feed your why, and do it.

There is a common saying: Don't sell the steak, sell the sizzle. Think of your why as a sizzle. Imagine a sizzle. What is it? Is it vegetables sizzling in a pan? Is it a big steak sizzling on a grill? The sound of a sizzle is enticing, and brings up an image of whatever that sizzle means to you. Have you ever been to a restaurant and heard a sizzle approach? What did you imagine it to be? Did it turn out to be something other than what you thought?

Your sizzle is what you are passionate about, and you need to be careful about the sizzle. You want to make sure it really is *Your Sizzle.* I'm talking about the difference of you motivating yourself versus others motivating you, like a positive motivational speaker or guru (or coach, as they now call themselves). These people sell sizzle. They sell a very compelling, very passionate story that gets you motivated.

Have you been to a positive motivational seminar? They get you hopping around, changing your state, and looking at ways more positive than you did before. When you leave, you are so motivated that you feel like you can move mountains.

But the reason the motivation doesn't last long is because it's their story, it's their sizzle: It's not yours. You want to find your sizzle. You want to find your own story. You need to define your own why. Don't let someone else's why run your life.

Ask yourself:

- Why am I doing what I am doing?
- What's behind that (especially if your first answer is $$)?

- What's behind that (No, this isn't a typo)? Keep going until you get to the core of your why.

Get specific. For instance:

Why do I want to work for a large corporation and make a minimum of $85,000 per year? (Of course, tailor this question to fit your situation)?

A why could be: "I want a lot of money." Great, what's behind that? "Well, when I was younger, my parents didn't have great jobs. We moved around a lot. We didn't have a lot of things we wanted, and I don't want that for my kids." Or "I don't want that for me." Fantastic!

That is great; you are getting a lot closer to your why. But, if you notice, this why is about stability at the core. Try not to make your why a negative. And yes, positive motivation plays a role here and it can help a great deal. Change your why from a negative to a positive.

The hardened criminal who had spent years killing young women didn't flinch at any of the speeches until Robert Rule, Linda's father, chose to forgive him. During Mr. Rule's speech of forgiveness, the killer broke down and cried.[8] A part of leadership is learning how to read people and help them to grow in unexpected ways. Mr. Rule influenced this person in a way that surprised everyone.

Survival of the fittest.

It's a dog-eat-dog world. Only the strongest survive. These are sayings that we know quite well. But are they actually true? Forgiveness can make a killer cry. We do better in groups than we do alone. There's even a chemical in the brain called oxytocin that makes us feel good when we help people that are less fortunate than we are.[9]

We would have masters and slaves if this were a survival of the fittest world. But God created us to care about our fellow man; so we work in social groups and strive to lift each other up.

For instance: Instead of "I don't want to live in a tent" say something like "I want to live in a comfortable house that gives me (or my family) safety." Instead of "I am tired of not having a job," maybe say something like "I want to provide a comfortable life for my family."

Some people will want to make a certain amount of money because they want to travel. Or, they may want to make money so they can help others that are less fortunate. And those are fantastic whys. In fact, the more your why helps others, the more likely it will come to pass. Remember the leadership drug in our brain called Oxytocin? It will help you accomplish your success planning, if your planning also helps others be successful.

When you ask why you are doing what you are doing, ask what's behind that. And, if you have a habit of not reaching your goals, if you are having difficulty figuring out what your why is, ask yourself if limiting beliefs are stopping you (remember when we talked about limiting beliefs in the Believe in Yourself section of Chapter 2?).

What are you passionate about? That could lead directly to your why. What gives you energy (aside from alone time)? What gets you out of bed in the morning?

\ \ \

Jason dreads getting out of bed, but only Monday through Friday because he "has" to work. Now, Friday is not so bad, but Monday's are the worst! He loves getting out of bed Saturday and Sunday (or staying in bed all day) because he doesn't have to work. Basically, he doesn't like his job, but it pays him very well.

\ \ \

My thought: Would I really want to be at a job that I hate, no matter how much it pays? Actually, I've been there and I left the job within a year. I couldn't keep working at a place that had different core beliefs (more on core beliefs in the next section, or go to www.webishops.com and look up Success Planning to watch the Core Beliefs Webishop) than I. Some people can do that, I cannot. It saps my energy. I have to do what I love to do, even if I get paid less to do it.

What saps your energy? This is another thing to look at while developing your why. As you determine the things that sap your energy, you will see things that are not your why, and knowing what is not your why will help you get to the core of what is your why.

What gives you energy? What gets you out of bed? What makes you look forward to the next day? That could be a part of your why.

For businesses:

Chances are, the people that work at a large corporation know what their particular job is, and they know what the corporation does. For instance, a person in a cotton factory may make cotton balls. When asked what they do, they can confidently say that they make cotton balls.

Their job is to make sure the cotton balls are as round as they can be (or whatever). The person next to him may make the bags that the cotton balls go into. She knows what she does and how to do it. And, it is important for the people in an organization to know how to do their particular job. If they don't know what they are doing, the product or service will not be done well.

It is also important that employees know how to do what they do. The person who is in charge of the cotton balls may need to constantly configure the machine so that the ball is round enough, and just the right amount of material is being used.

The person overseeing the bag making machine needs to make sure the seams are correct and the bags are the right size. If a person does not know how to do what they are doing, it's definitely a training issue (or possibly time to free up that person's future).

Most people in most organizations know what they do, and they know how to do it. But, most people in most organizations do not know why they do what they do. Most people just do it for the paycheck. Even the CEOs of some companies are working for a paycheck. This is very common in businesses where you have a second or third generation person running the company.

I'm going to pick on Ford. Ford motor company became a great corporation. Henry Ford did a good job growing his company. He had a definite, specific why for Ford Motor company. However, when he passed away and his heirs took over, the company didn't do as well. They didn't have the Why that Henry had.

Organizations very often struggle with generational issues. When the generation that figured out the why turns over the company, and the next generation comes in, they quite often do not have the same why. And, if they don't figure out their own why, a why that ties in with the original, then statistically they are not going to last. There will be exceptions to the rule, but that is generally what happens.

For instance, if you make pencils because your father made pencils, not having a solid why may not destroy the corporation because people still need pencils. But, if you are the child of the founder, why are you doing it? Is it just because dad did it?

A good example of this is in the movie *Iron Man*™. Tony Stark, toward the beginning of the movie, says something to the effect that his father did it, he is doing it now, it works, so let's keep doing it. But he is talking about weapons of mass destruction, and he didn't have a solid why.

So, when one of his own weapons changed his life, he changed his tune and decided not to make weapons anymore. Yes, this is fantasy, but it is a good point. He created a new *why* that he could live by, and he changed the company that he was running because of that. Changing the Why may change the company. But if you are the person running the company, that's okay because you have to have your own why.

Core Values

Talking about core values isn't really a sexy type of discussion like the vision or the mission ones are these days, so I'm very glad you took the time to read this. I highly recommend determining what your core values are or, what do you believe in?

Are you ready for that kind of a religious discussion? And if you're not, good: This isn't a religious discussion. If you are a religious person your values will probably tie in with that, but your core values do not have to have anything to do with any particular religion. Your core values do, however, tie in with your why.

Your core values define you even when you have not defined them.

What are core values? To answer that question, let's look at what core values are not. First they're not mission statements (your mission, or edict, is the next section) and they're not vision statements. Your core values are not your why but your core values do tie in, like I said, with your why to be your foundation.

They're not your strategy, your core values are not your day to day working schedule. They're not your target market. However, your core values will help determine your edict, vision, strategy and your target market.

Your core values will help you define what your edict (mission) is. When you say your edict is to do X and you already know what your core values are, it becomes that much easier to define X. When you see the results of your vision in your head, it will be easier to accomplish that vision when it is in line with your core values.

And the same holds true for your strategy and target market. The only item that is not driven by your core values is your why. However, your why and core values should align perfectly. If they do not, something went wrong in the planning process. Were you listening to the wrong voices in your head?

For some strange reason, introverts seem to have more of a dialog in their heads than extroverts (and no, extroverts, that is NOT proof that we are crazy). I feel for you if you are prone to negative self-talk, and maybe I can help. The next time you find negative self-talk taking over, try these two things:

Change your posture. If you are sitting, jump up (if nobody is watching), sit up straighter, do something physically different and then make a silly smiley face.

Tell yourself that is the old you. The new you does not want that anymore, and turn the negative thought into a positive thought. Remind yourself that the new you is a positive thinker.

Yes, it sounds silly. But you have nothing to lose and a whole new way of looking at life to gain.

One common definition of core values is: Core values are commonly held beliefs and commitments. However, core values are personal, so you could say that your core values are what define you, or what define your business.

Most people and most businesses have arbitrary core values; meaning that they have not specifically defined their core values so those values can change based on how you or the business is doing or on how the CEO feels.

But that could be a recipe for disaster. As an example, let's say you get a job offer from a company that wants to give you a larger salary and a signing bonus. That may seem amazing on the surface. In fact, I've had that happen myself and it did look amazing so I took the offer. I made a lot of money, and for a year I hated going to work because my core values did not align with the business's core values.

I did not have my core values written down, they were not specifically defined, and I did not know what the business's core values were either. If I would have written mine down and compared it with theirs, I would have known right up front that I would not be happy there because their core values were basically that their employees were very well paid slaves.

When something went wrong, everyone had to stay until it was fixed, no matter how long it took. They paid overtime, and the money was great, but nobody could leave without permission at times. Some of the people there accepted that, but I could not. I had a family that was important to me.

It is important to have written down specific core values. Your why and your core values work together, like I mentioned, to be the foundation for your life, your family, your team, your business, your organization, or whatever it might be.

You may have separate core values for each of them, but you will find that the core values for each item fall in line with the others. They will all be similar and, if they're not similar, that may be an area of your life that isn't working so well. This is an opportunity to take the Path of Life assessment at the back of this book to see which areas of your life need the most work.

\` \` \`

Jay had a good life. He got along well with his family, had a great job and was heading in the direction he wanted. But his personal relationships didn't last long. He had such a difficult time dating that he was about ready to give up.

However, as he worked on his core values, he realized that the way he acted toward women was not the same as he expected them to act toward him. And, the way he acted did not align with his core values either. But, he hadn't realized it because he hadn't actually written them down before.

\` \` \`

Jay spent some time writing down his core values and the core values he would like to see in a girlfriend. I won't say that Jay magically met the love his life the next day, but he does have a new, more positive outlook on relationships now.

Keep that in mind as you start to work on the core values of different areas of your life. Think about which areas of your life that are not in balance. If your life isn't working as well as you want in some areas, and you look at how that area of your life is going versus the core values you defined for that area, you might figure out why.

Once you determine your why and start to define your core values, you will have a better idea of what culture you fit into.

Your why and your core values help you determine your culture. Is it a laid-back culture? Is it a high-demand culture? Is it a run till you drop culture? Is it a quick high-five then on to the next vision culture? Is it a party with every success culture? What is your culture?

And when you know your core values, you will know the right tribe to join (or lead). You will know the right career. You will know the right people to bring into your business. You will know how to guide your family.

Remember how I talked about the company that I worked for whose core values didn't align with mine? I disliked working there. I didn't know why I didn't like it; the people were nice and it was a huge company. It paid well and had good working conditions. I had not defined my core values, but my core values had defined me. So I didn't know consciously what they were, but they were telling me that something was not right.

Are you working off false assumptions? Are false assumptions where your values are coming from? Or are they possibly coming from a place of fear? That is not necessarily a bad thing. Fear is a natural response to imminent danger.

There may have been something that happened in your past, and fear is telling you that this is a similar situation. You could have core values based off that fear, but fear is an emotion that we need to control, or it will control us. Have you ever been frozen from fear? Or panicked and done something completely different from your character?

\ \ \

When I was 8 years old my parents took my sister and I to visit family in the Midwest. Early one morning I went with my cousin on his paper route. It was a dark and foggy morning.

That sounds like the start of a mystery novel, doesn't it? And, true to the mystery novel, we got separated. I found myself in a strange city, not knowing where I was or where I needed to go. I panicked. Fear told me to run, so I did. I ended up several miles away from where I was supposed to be.

I blindly ran across intersections several times, not thinking to check to see if cars were coming. In fact, fear probably caused me more danger than I would have been in if I had controlled my fear.

\ \ \

Do not let fear dictate your core values.

Maybe your core values are coming from a place of hope. Perhaps you see yourself a multi-millionaire in the near future; owning a huge house and nice cars, with good looking men or women hanging off your arms. Maybe you see rainbows and unicorns and know nothing can go wrong.

But, just as it is unwise to let fear define your core values, be careful of hope also. I recommend that your core values come from a place of positive expectancy. Hope is there, but not in control. Fear may be there as well, and possibly should be if you are stretching yourself.

But fear is not in control either. You expect positive things to happen and you know that there will be setbacks also. Your why and your core values are the solid foundation for your better tomorrow. With them, you will be better prepared for the setbacks. And besides, what are setbacks really but springboards to the next level? The only time a setback becomes a failure is if you quit.

There is a big difference between hope and expectancy. Hope to me is *pie in the sky*, as in; it's not defined. It's fluffy clouds; it's something that might or might not happen. But expectancy, when you expect something to happen, has a greater chance of happening. So think about your core values as coming from a place of positive expectancy.

Why spend time working on core values? They will help with every decision you make; they help make decisions easier, quicker and with less confusion, and you're generally happier once you've made those decisions.

What are the core values of the company for which you currently work? If you run the company, ask the employees what they think the core values are and see if they align with what you want them to be.

How about the core values of your relationship? Have you had that discussion with your significant other? Do you need to talk to your kids about the family core values? What are your personal core values? Do they line up with all the above?

Determining your core values may change the way you do things. A lady down south had a goal to make a million dollars within three years. However, while working on her core values she remembered that she had a passion for working with at-risk teens.

Now, I can tell you that at-risk teens don't generally have a million dollars lying around to pay people. So, sometimes you may need to adjust your wants so you can also work on your passions. It's okay to want money, but will the money make you happy? There is more than one lottery winner that has committed suicide.[1]

If you have a difficult time making decisions, it could be because your core values are too arbitrary. How do you figure out what your core values are? That part is pretty simple. I've designed a core values worksheet which is in Appendix 1. Or, you can download and print it out. Just go to www.webishops.com/successplanning. You will find the link to the worksheet under the Core Values Webishop video.

The worksheet has a large list of core values and there are instructions on how to determine what yours are. It is not difficult, but make sure you do it (if you want, you can do the core values worksheet as part of your Getaway, found at the end of this chapter).

Don't copy someone else's core values, even if they seem similar, because they are not. Every person is different, and nobody thinks exactly like you do, so don't let someone else determine your core values. Define your core values for your family, for your business or career, for your life. It can make such a huge difference in everything that you do, and can make decisions much easier.

Once you know why you do what you do, and what your core values are, take a closer look at what you do.

Your Mission | What Do You Do?

The why and core values are the being part of success planning. We are human beings, but we like doing more than we like being because doing is tangible. We can touch and feel the things that we do; but we cannot really touch and feel the being side, so we don't put as much of an importance to it.

And that is exactly where you can outshine others. Being is half of the equation. If you can understand that part of the equation better than most people, you have just raised your value to the world.

But that was the last two sections. Now, we are on to doing. What are you doing or; what is your mission? What is your royal decree? Those are actually two separate things, and we will get into both of them.

The absence of, or poorly written, Vision and Mission statements are lost opportunities for:

- Attracting/engaging/retaining talent
- Building organizational culture
- Increasing *productivity* while leveraging all resources to successfully implement a strategic plan."– Janell Evans[2]

Your mission answers the question; what do you do? And it begs the question; is that really what you do (I know this sounds a lot like why, but it turns left soon)? Mission is a part of doing. Your mission is part of the action.

For example: Let's say John Jacob Jingleheimer Schmidt works in a factory. He stands at a conveyor belt. His job is to put nuts and bolts into compartment B of a container so the product that this company makes will have all of its nuts and bolts for the customer when it gets shipped out.

When people ask, he says: “My job is to stand at a conveyor belt. I'm putting nuts and bolts into container B and that's what I do all day long. It’s kind of boring, but...”

Is that really what he does? Maybe on the surface; but looking more closely we see that he has to put the right size nuts and bolts into the right container. He then needs to make sure that the correct number of nuts and bolts is there before he goes on to the next set. So, in reality, he doesn't put nuts and bolts in the container as much as he is a part of the customer satisfaction experience of the company.

He's also a part of quality control. So, he can wake up each morning and say "okay, here I go. I get to put nuts and bolts into a container again all day long," or he can wake up each morning and say "I want to make sure these customers have the best satisfaction possible with our product. I can help with the quality control as well, and in doing that I'm making sure that two bolts go in the container."

You can talk about what you are doing from one point of view, but can you see how his mission could be one of quality control and customer satisfaction also?

Getting to the core of what you do is similar to getting to the core of why. You need to know what it is you do before you can create a mission statement.

Two Types of Mission Statements

There are two types of mission statements: The twentieth century mission statement and the twenty-first century edict, or the royal decree. And it is very important to look at the differences between the two. Your standard twentieth century mission statement is about what you do or what you want to do. It's not too specific, and remember; mission statements do not have end dates.

The mission statement should be something that will live the life of your corporation, organization, team, family or whatever it might be. This is not written in stone, however. Everything changes. So don't fret if you decide to change your mission statement, just don't do so lightly.

The mission statement should be brief. Your mission should not be more than 30 words or a couple of paragraphs at most (if you think this is short, wait until I talk about the Edict). The mission statement is your statement to the world about what you do or what you want to do. It's in alignment with your why, core values, target market, strategic vision and your strategy. They all come together for one big Success Plan.

A good mission statement will stimulate the mind and the imagination. The mission statement should not be boring, bland or generic. Make it your own. It needs to fit the culture of your company.

So, what goes into creating a good mission statement? I have included several examples of good (and not so good) mission statements, with comments, in Appendix 3. You want to stimulate the imagination if you can, even if you have a mundane business model.

The first thing you need to define is what type of mission statement is it is: Is it for the entire organization if you have a large organization; is it a regional mission statement, for a department, or a specific team?

Is it a family mission statement or is it a mission statement just for you? Yes, you should have mission statements for each, but pick your battles. Which is the most important to do first?

I recommend that everybody write down their personal mission statement first. Just like your why, you could be roped into following someone else's mission if you don't know your own.

The next step in developing your mission statement is determining who's going to help; who is going to be part of the team (if you will have a team. Read the mission statement part of the Getaway at the end of this chapter for recommended steps on developing your mission statement). Are you going to have a leadership team or a management team? Will the entire department or organization be a part of it?

If it's a family mission statement, will it be the husband and the wife or will the children be involved? You could even include the infant if you truly want buy-in from everyone.

Infants are a lot like introverts; they don't say too much, but when they do talk it's very important to listen, and they tell you how important it is because if you don't listen to them they start crying (infants, not introverts). Of course some adults will start crying when you don't listen also, but that's an issue for coaching, so we will stick to the mission statement for now.

- What do you do?
- What do you really do?
- What do you want to do?
- What type of business (or organization) is it?

Remember John, the guy that stands at the conveyor belt putting bolts in a compartment? The physical aspect of what you do (putting bolts into a compartment) could be different from what you really do (provide customer satisfaction and quality control).

Designing Your Mission Statement

Get group input and buy-in when determining what your mission statement is, but do not design the actual mission statement by committee. The principle stakeholder should have the final say in the mission statement.

There is a reason for this: When a mission statement is designed by committee, every person will want their word put into it. So, if you have a business or department of 60 people, your mission statement will invariably be at least 60 words long.

Your mission is your statement to the world about what you do. It's not your statement to yourself (unless it is your personal mission statement). Write it down so the whole organization/team has access to it. You will not have a defined mission until it's written down. That is very important, so grab that pen and paper, your tablet, your computer, whatever it might be. Get it written down.

Mission Statement Development Steps:

1. Is it a mission statement or edict?
2. What type of business (or organization) is it?
3. Who will be part of the development?
4. Who will be the main decision maker (stakeholder)?
5. What do you do?
6. What do you really do?
7. What do you want to do?

The mission needs to be a statement that everyone can get behind, so be sure to develop one that is in line with your culture (remember, your culture is defined by your why and core values).

> *Keep in mind that, while everyone needs to get behind it, not everyone has to be happy with your mission.*

Write down everything you can think of in developing your mission statement or edict. It does not matter how long it is for now, you will edit it later.

Once it's written down, shorten it. Mission statements, when they're first written down, can be very long and very cumbersome. It's pretty easy to shorten them and you want to make it memorable. The shorter it is, the more likely people will read it, and the more memorable it will be.

Think about who you are targeting with this mission statement. Who is your target audience or your target market? How are you serving them? Think about that when you're shortening your mission statement.

A mission statement that never gets looked at is useless, even if it's written down. My first attempt at Success Planning was with a company I started many years ago. I gathered the board of directors together and we designed a mission statement.

We spent several hours trying to figure out the exact words we wanted and came away with an awesome, fantastic mission statement that we were proud of. I quickly scribbled the final product at the bottom of a page in my notebook.

I told myself that I would make it more official soon, and promptly forgot about it. I went searching for the notebook several months later, but it had grown legs and wandered off. I still haven't found that mission statement to this day, over a decade later.

So make sure that it gets put into a place where you can find it. Don’t design it and put it away, put it on display. Get it in emails; get it on the wall of the office or the lunchroom. Whatever it might be, make sure everybody knows what it is because if they don't look at it, it's useless. The mission statement is one of the pieces that are going to help unify everybody toward your shared vision (which is the next section).

Your Edict

I have been an entrepreneur most of my life. Part of the life of an entrepreneur is to attend business networking events (I feel you introverts shivering, I do too). Developing an elevator pitch, or a description of what you do that can be said within 30 seconds (the time it takes to go a couple of floors in an elevator) is one of the best things you can do to make an impact during these events.

I had a radical idea; what if a mission statement could be said in 30 seconds. Then I remembered something I heard a long time ago; keep removing words until it stops making sense. So, what if a mission statement could be said in six words or less? Would it even be a mission statement at that point?

And what would be a better way to describe it? A word that sparks imagination itself, something that is enticing. A word that shows how important the statement is: An edict, which is a Royal Decree, sounded pretty good to me.

Can you describe what you do in six words or less? It almost sounds overwhelming on the surface, but I believe in you.

Your edict should be designed after, not instead of, your mission statement. Yes, your edict may replace your mission statement, but it is easy to mess up an edict if you do not have your mission defined.

For instance, as I wrote in the beginning of this book, 85% of businesses have not gone through Success Planning, so they do not have a defined mission. I have helped many businesses with this process. And when I start working with them, I ask them what they do.

Many service oriented business owners I have spoken to have given me the same answer: "I help people." I have gotten that answer from attorneys and massage therapists and counselors. It would be too easy to design a generic edict, like "I help people," if the mission statement is not properly defined, so please do not skip that step.

I call the edict the 21st century mission statement because we keep making things shorter. If you go back in written history, you will find that people used to use a lot more words. The Old Testament of the Bible, for instance, would have been shrunk by half if it were written by someone today.

In fact, words were used so much in the distant past that it was common to say the same thing three times if it was important. Of course, most people could not read back then so stories were memorized and repeated over and over. It would make sense to say something three times if someone wanted to be sure other people were going to remember it.

Now an emoticon says everything. Gone are the days of the long, drawn out acronym (lol, brb, etc.). The old saying "a picture is worth a thousand words" is becoming more true every day. So it seems fitting that the days of the emoticon are also the days of the edict.

Designing Your Edict

Your edict is a massively shrunk mission statement. Your mission statement is probably two or more paragraphs right now, which is fine. A mission statement uses a lot of words to say what it means, which started reminding me of the Tree Ents in the movie *Lord of the Rings* after I designed my first edict.

Treebeard, the main Tree Ent of the movie, tells two Hobbits that it takes a very long time to say anything in all Entish, and Ents do not say anything unless it takes a very long time to say.

Start dissecting your mission statement. Take out words that are not needed (there are usually a few). Keep taking out words that are not needed, but make sure your mission statement still makes sense.

This process could take several hours, days, or even weeks so do not get discouraged if it does not turn out correctly the first time. Keep at it, and get help if you need it. A fresh pair of eyes and a new perspective may not hurt.

Example Edicts

I do not know of many edicts out there, so I am going to make a few up.

There was a college football player who got tired of his clothes sticking to him when he sweated, so he decided to design a line of clothing that got moisture away from the skin. An edict for that company could be as simple as "we create moisture-wicking clothing."

The most popular hamburger restaurant on the planet could have an edict of "fast food."

There is another popular hamburger restaurant that starts with a W. Their food is reportedly a bit better for you than the restaurant that starts with an M, so their edict could be "healthier fast food."

Your edict is the service you provide, boiled down to its most base element.

At MyCoach.Life, our edict is "unlocking potential."

The sports clothing company who has a swoop for a logo could have the edict of "athletic apparel."

Your edict should be no more than six words, and as many less as you can. How much easier is it to make it memorable? You can give somebody a three paragraph mission statement and say this is our mission. It might be an amazing mission statement, but chances are the first time reading it they're not going to remember what it said. You may not remember it.

You, your staff, and your clients will remember something like "moisture-wicking clothing." And the reason is obvious: It's simple. So whenever anyone asks what you do, you could pull out a three paragraph mission statement or quickly tell them your edict (you don't have to get into the conversation of an edict versus a mission statement if you don't want to).

Your Strategic Vision | Where Are You Going?

Your mind works in pictures (and movies).[3] Think about it, if someone asks where you live, a picture of your residence pops into your mind. If they ask where you work, you see a picture of your workspace.

Even if a person is asked what something smells like, they remember the smell then see a picture of the food. That is why your vision of the future is so important. If you can see where you want to be in vivid detail, your mind will work to get you there. The only question is . . .

What is stopping you from creating your compelling strategic vision? Is it:

- Time?
- Money?
- Help from others?
- Fear?
- Knowledge / information?
- Something else?

I would say that fear is the #1 reason more people do not accomplish the vision for their lives.[4] Fear can be crippling and devastating. For introverts, the fear of knowing we have to leave our safe havens and go socialize can be a huge reason that stops us. We can use the other items on the list as excuses, but most of the time it boils down to fear.

Think about it, if you knew for 100% certainty that you had a product or service which every angel investor in your area would be fighting for; if you had the next guaranteed million dollar idea, you could find the money. Or you could find someone to fund your idea if you didn't have the money yourself. You would find the time if you knew you would make a million dollars. There would be little fear in asking for help. And knowledge is rarely a factor in the age of the Internet.

It is the fear of *not* being sure it will work that stops us most of the time. It is that nagging doubt in the back of your mind, wondering if anyone would ever hire you, come into your store, or read that book you are so excited to write.

What if it does not work? What if, despite your best efforts, nobody comes to your web site? Or worse, what if thousands go to your web site but your phone never rings? Or the innovation you came up with sits in a garage because no sales are coming through? Does just the thought of that make your self-confidence sink to the floor? That is fear.

And fear is very real. Some people use this acronym for fear:

False Evidence Appearing Real.

The last two words are huge: APPEARING REAL. Ever have someone jump out and scare the living daylights out of you? The evidence was false, they were not going to hurt you, but it sure Appeared Real in that instance, didn't it?!

However, after you gave your friend or family member some "physical education," you got over it and moved on with your day. Although it appeared real in the moment, you later realized it was false.

The alternative is letting fear freeze you, and your life not changing. But you are not reading this book because you want to stay where you are. You have conquered a part of your fear just by reading this far. Give yourself a pat on the back; you have already taken a step forward. Conquering fear is like eating an elephant. You just have to do it one bite at a time.

What would your vision of the future be if nothing could stop you? What if you had the time, money, knowledge, assistance, and fear was not a factor? Where would you be in 90 days, six months, or five years? What would that look like? Answering these questions is the beginning of your strategic vision.

But what is a strategic vision? Why is it important and what are the steps to creating one?

A strategic vision is one that answers the question "where am I (are we) going?" Answering this question is important because you will never get to your destination if you don't know where it is.

A ship going from New York to London may crash into the shore if the GPS is off by one tick. However, even with GPS a ship can go off course due to tides, wind, and weather. Constant course corrections are needed whenever you captain a ship. And, like a ship, your strategic vision will need constant course corrections (more on that in the Game Plan section).

That is also one of the reasons why a strategic vision is important. Along with clarifying the direction, a strategic vision will provide clarity of purpose; it will create passion, it augments leadership, and it gives permission to take risks.

There are five steps to creating a strategic vision (plus one bonus). They are:

1. Be precise
2. Define your timeframe
3. Determine the necessary steps
4. Make sure it is feasible
5. Keep it realistic

I scoured the Internet for a good example of a strategic vision statement. I could not find one in any of the company or organizations I searched (see Appendix 3 for some examples of vision statements that were not so good).

I did, however, find an amazing vision statement from an unlikely source. It comes from President Kennedy's speech at Rice University on September 12, 1962. It was his speech about America putting a man on the moon, and it has all the elements of a great strategic vision.[5]

Do an Internet search for "Kennedy Moon Speech" if you would like to watch or read it. I am just going to show the parts that make up the strategic vision aspect (each of the areas in quotes are directly from President Kennedy).

\ \ \

"We choose to go to the moon in this decade."

President Kennedy started his strategic vision exactly how any strategic vision should begin; he specifically stated where he wanted to go (step 1) and when it would be done by (step 2).

Every strategic vision has an end date. There will come a time when the vision turns into reality. If a vision is never designed to become reality, it is just a dream.

". . . we shall send to the moon, 240,000 miles away from the control station in Houston, a giant rocket more than 300 feet tall, the length of this football field, made of new metal alloys, some of which have not yet been invented. . ."

Do not let limitations stop you from designing your strategic vision. Make the incorporation of overcoming those limitations part of your vision. That is what makes it strategic. A good strategic vision will list obstacles, and how you will overcome them. In fact, I would say this is one of the base qualities of a leader; seeing the obstacles and finding ways of overcoming them before they happen.

Step 5 in designing your vision is asking yourself if your vision is realistic. Can it be done with what you already have and know? President Kennedy freely admitted that the rocket to the moon would use materials that have not been invented, but that does not make his vision a dream.

Both America and Russia had already sent animals into Earth's orbit,[6] so he knew it could be done. However, he wanted it known that it would be done better and safer than how it had been performed in the past.

"However, I think we're going to do it, and I think that we must pay what needs to be paid. I don't think we ought to waste any money, but I think we ought to do the job."

Kennedy was establishing feasibility, step 4 in designing a strategic vision. He was telling America that it was going to cost a lot of money, but that it would be worth it to America.

"During the next 5 years the National Aeronautics and Space Administration expects to double the number of scientists and engineers in this area, to increase its outlays for salaries and expenses to $60 million a year; to invest some $200 million in plant and laboratory facilities; and to direct or contract for new space efforts over $1 billion from this Center in this City."

\ \ \

Step 3 of developing your strategic vision is determining what steps you are going to take. This last quote is more of an overview, but it serves its purpose. You should have more detail for your strategy, but I highly recommend developing a strategic vision similar to President Kennedy's speech.

Step 1: Be Precise

Where exactly do you see yourself? What do you want to say about yourself that you cannot say now? Where do you want your business, job, team, or organization to be in the future? How clear is that vision?

Clarity is important. You need to keep envisioning the future until all the clouds are gone and you can count every blade of grass. Okay, maybe not that specific. God may know every hair on our heads, but that doesn't mean we need to.

However, you do want to have a clear vision. Being Precise = clarity. Be clear on what you want. When you have clarity it creates passion, not only in yourself but in the other people that are involved.

Whether it is an organization, a business, a team, a ministry, a family; even if it's your own personal vision, it needs to create passion in the people that it affects. It's also going to clarify direction.

You can have the fastest plane in the world, but it's not going to matter if you don't know where you're going. Chances are you're going to get lost really quick.

> *License Plate Surround: "I don't know where I'm going, but I'm making good time."*

But clarifying direction will augment leadership. The people below you, the members of your team (unless this is a personal vision in which case you are your own leader), will more likely follow a leader that has a clear vision.

In fact, an article in Inc. Magazine stated that the #3 reason people will leave a job, even when they like it, is due to a vague vision.[7]

Being precise, having a clear vision, also allows risk-taking from those under you. Let's say you're managing a medium-sized organization and you have a team of leaders below you. If they don't know where the organization is going, they're not going to take risks on getting there. How can you take a risk on getting somewhere if you don't know where that is?

What if an employee takes a risk and it's the wrong risk because it ends up going in the wrong direction? Is that the fault of the employee for going in the wrong direction, or the fault of the leader for not providing a clear strategic vision?

Step one in creating your strategic vision: Be precise, precise to the head of a pin if you can do it. I've coached people that have said "I want to be rich." Well, what does rich look like to you? Everybody in America is rich compared to most of the world. There are children in India that live on the trash homeless people in America throw away.

Maybe you want forty percent more net income by the end of the year. That is a pretty good definition, but it could be more precise. Where will that net income come from? Will it be a raise? Will it be new customers? Will it be add on sales to existing customers or adding on a new product line or service? Will it be developing a new company?

Maybe you want to go on vacation. Where do you want to go? Don't say "the tropics." Again, be as precise as you can. Don't even say "Hawaii." If your destination is Hawaii, be specific. Say that you want to stay at a hotel right on Waikiki beach. Or you want to be in a condo in the middle of the rain forest on Kauai. Better yet, write down the name of the condo or hotel in which you want to stay.

Use descriptive words when writing down your vision. The more colorful the picture, the more you will be able to see yourself accomplishing it. Dr. Malphurs, author of *Developing a Vision for Ministry* indicates that expressive language is a . . . "Powerful tool in the hands of visionary leaders."[8]

Think of a GPS coordinate. Imagine you're on a ship and you say "hey I'm going to sail from Florida to England." England isn't that small of a country and there are many ports along the coast.

There are also many miles of coastline that have no ports. You probably want to sail to a port so that you can get off your ship when you get there, so you'll need to know the GPS coordinate of that port. To say "I'm sailing to England" isn't going to be enough. You could get to England by following compass directions or the stars; but if you had a GPS location you would get exactly where you're going much easier. So be precise.

Step 2: Your Timeframe

What is your timeframe? How do you determine your timeframe? Many of the people I coach think they can do more with their time than they can (and, as a matter of fact, I am guilty of that myself sometimes).

They are not being unrealistic; they just forget how many time suckers we have in a day. Kids, bills, television, friends, lazy time, coffee breaks (and on) will all take time. And, if all that takes time out of your day, how much time is taking out of your week?

That does not mean that you need to send your kids to an orphanage or unfriend everyone from social media (no matter how enticing that may seem). You just need to be realistic with your time.

Add in fudge factors to the time you think it will take you to do tasks. If it will take two hours a day for three months to reach your vision, plan on three hours a day. Or, if you don't have more than two hours available, plan on four months. It is better for your self-esteem if you plan on more time and finish early than planning on less time and finishing late.

Step 3: Determine the Necessary Steps

Once you have figured out your timeframe, determine what steps you need to take to get there (these can be the same as the major milestones in your game plan in the next section). Think of your strategic vision. If you want to do X and you want to do it by the end of the year, determine what the first step will be to get there.

> *Hey, we're introverts and that means we are creative. You don't have to start with the first step. Another option is to start with your end vision and work backward. As an example, maybe your strategic vision is to have a group of ten people*

working together on a project within two years. What is the last step you would need to take? Once you figure that out, look at the step before that and so on. Just don't start in the middle.

\ \ \

Nick has been in the restaurant industry for years. Now he has decided to stretch his entrepreneurial muscles and strike out on his own by opening an Italian restaurant. His strategic vision is to open within 12 months. And within 12 months after that he plans to have a certain number of customers per day, with each customer spending a certain amount of money.

\ \ \

There are actually two different visions here. The first is to open the restaurant. That can be a big task itself, so it's better to split this up. The second vision will be for the income. Each of these two visions can interact, though. For instance, Nick might start marketing his restaurant before it opens to generate interest.

The reason for two different visions is because it may be feasible to have the number of customers he wants within 12 months, but what if the permitting process delays the opening of the restaurant? This way, setbacks in one vision will not make more work for the other vision.

Being precise, setting the timeframe, and determining the necessary steps may make you think that the last two steps are not necessary, but they are. Once the first three steps are complete, find out if your strategic vision is feasible and realistic.

Step 4: Is It Feasible

Stacy had a vision to be a millionaire, and she knew she could do it. She wanted a net worth of exactly one million dollars by the end of the year. She determined if she could buy and flip just three of the right houses in that amount of time, she would have enough to purchase two more houses, fix them up and rent them out. Each of the two houses she would rent out would be worth over $500,000. She even had the first three houses already picked out.

Stacy's vision was clear. It was precise, she had the timeline down, and she already had most of the steps detailed out on how she would do it. Most, but not all.

Stacy had no idea how she was going to get the money to buy the first three houses. She wasn't working at the time, and had less than $1,000 to her name. She was determined, though, and wanted to go to banks to get a loan.

But Stacy also had no experience in flipping houses. Her history was with fast food restaurants, and she admittedly had only swung a hammer a few times in her life.

Could Stacy achieve her vision? Of course, it's been done before under more difficult circumstances. But, is it feasible? I don't like to burst bubbles, but during a coaching session I would ask Stacy about the importance of accomplishing this vision in less than 12 months.

This could be a more strategic vision if she designed it to purchase and flip one house, no matter how much money she got out of it. That way she could determine how long it would actually take, what obstacles she would need to overcome that she doesn't even know about right now, etc.

Is your strategic vision feasible with your skill set? Will it work with your family situation? You may have a vision to jet-set around the world, but if you are in the middle-income bracket and have two children in school, is it feasible?

Take a realistic look at your life right now. Is every aspect of your strategic vision feasible within that setting? If not, what will need to change to make it happen and are you willing to make that change? You may realize that you have designed the vision you will need *after* the vision you need now, and that's okay.

Step 5: Realistic

Sometimes, even when a vision is feasible, it is not realistic.

Looking back at Stacy from the last step; even if it were feasible to flip three houses in less than 12 months, is it realistic? What if she wanted to keep as much money as possible, so she did almost all the work herself and found out that she would need to work 16 hours days, 7 days a week, in order to accomplish it? Is that feasible?

Yes, she would still have eight hours a day to sleep, but is that realistic? She would have no life, she would probably lose touch with most of her friends, and don't forget the old adage "all work and no play..."

Think of the last resolution you made, was it realistic? How about the last goal you had for yourself, your family, or your career? Did you set the goal so high that there was no way to realistically achieve it?

Did you do that because, on some level, you didn't believe you could achieve it anyway?

This is your chance to take a last, hard look at your strategic vision. A strategic vision is designed to stretch you, to help you grow. But it cannot be designed to break you.

And, a strategic vision should not be designed as a dream. "Someday Isle" is not your destination. Your vision must have an end date. Yes, things happen, and maybe you will need to adjust that end date. But create a realistic end date for the vision.

Bonus: Obstacles

Congratulations! You discovered the Super-Secret area that will help propel your strategic vision! If you *really* want to have a vision that is more likely to succeed, determine what obstacles you are going to come across, and develop a plan on how to get around them.

There are a lot of authors that talk about the importance of vision, and many people talk about the steps to determine the vision. However, very few people talk about obstacles. But it is so important because obstacles are going to bang on your *fear button*; especially when you're not planning for them.

Think of the last time you encountered an obstacle you didn't plan for. Maybe it was a layoff, a large customer that suddenly went somewhere else, a car accident, a team member that left, a financial crisis, or a business partner that backed out. Did you suddenly feel overwhelmed, like life, that unfair being, was purposefully holding you back? Did you start to let depression take over?

Now think about the last obstacle that you did plan for. Maybe you checked the traffic before you left for work and found a huge obstacle like a fallen tree on the main road you travel. So, you took an alternate route. Maybe you got to work a couple of minutes late, but you still made better time that if you had not checked the traffic.

How did that make you feel? Maybe you were still frustrated, but it is no reason to beat yourself up. In fact, you may have secretly congratulated yourself for anticipating the obstacle and overcoming it.

\ \ \

Jim is a salesman that goes to customers on a daily basis. He has a vision; he has his timeframe and he knows the steps he wants to take. It is feasible and realistic. Then his car breaks down.

That's an obstacle that stops him dead in his tracks. Without a car he cannot get to appointments or meet with new customers. But Jim wrote "car breaking down" as a possible obstacle when he designed his vision. He has an app for local bus routes and he knows about rideshare programs and taxis in his city.

He also has written down the name of a repair shop he will take his car to because it is run by a man he knows and trusts. Jim planned for obstacles in his strategic vision and it benefited him.

\ \ \

Do you see what a great advantage it can be to look at the possible obstacles, list them, and determine how to overcome them? A car breaking down is stressful in the best of times, but much more so when your livelihood depends on it. Jim just lowered his stress level a great deal by having alternatives ready before the obstacle happened.

There is another advantage to this step: As you work on how to overcome obstacles, more obstacles may come to mind. Work on how to overcome them as well. You are teaching your mind that obstacles are there to be conquered.

Then fear will not freeze you if an obstacle occurs that you didn't think of; you have taught yourself the steps to take to work on overcoming it. Obstacles are the pathway to opportunity; and the conquest of today's obstacle could be your next big idea.

You can be successful without completing your vision. Let's say your vision is to feed 500 people in need over the next 6 months, but after that amount of time you only fed 100.

There is a level of success to that. Or let's say your vision is to grow your business by 60% over the next 12 months. You tried new marketing techniques, designed new sales goals for the staff, and implemented new ideas.

But your business only grew 10%. That is still successful. You learned many new things about what to do, and what not to do. Success doesn't mean you actually accomplish the vision, so don't beat yourself up if everything doesn't go your way. Adjust your vision and start again.

Sharing Your Vision

Your strategic vision (unless it is a personal vision) should not be kept to yourself. The best vision is one that is shared with everyone involved, if you want it to be successful. But share everything, not just the vision statement. Let everyone know why you are doing it, what your core values are, your edict (or mission), the vision, and the game plan.

Get buy-in from those below you. Listen to their concerns and take them into consideration. If you are in upper management and you designed a vision that includes the people actually doing the work, listen to what they have to say.

They are the ones on the ground floor; they work daily on things you may have forgotten about. Talk to the sales team, get buy in from support. Find a way to make it *their* vision and they will work hard to accomplish it.

The Vision Hack

As I said at the beginning of this section, your mind works in pictures and your mind works to accomplish what you think about the most. Would you like a way to hack your mind to help it accomplish that vision?

Maybe your vision is to live in a beautiful house in a certain neighborhood. Find a picture of the house you want, or one as close to it as you can, and Photoshop your (or your family's) picture onto it. Then print that image out and tape it to your mirror so you see it every time you go into the bathroom. Not only will your mind see the house you want, it will see you at that house.

If your vision is a new car, do the same thing. If you want to be a successful sales person, find a picture that conveys the feeling and paste your portrait onto it. Do the same thing no matter what your vision is. If your vision is to go back to school, paste a picture of yourself in a classroom.

This hack is more difficult if your vision is 40% higher returns in sales over last year, but that is a difficult thing for the mind to turn into a picture anyway. So think about what you will do with that money. Will you help homeless people, go on a mission to help an African tribe, redo your kitchen, hire more staff or move to a bigger office? Find a vision that can be translated to a picture.

But what if you are not good at cutting and pasting on a computer? What if you have no idea what to do? That's the real hack. Go to a site like fiverr.com or upwork.com and hire a freelancer to do it for you. Just give them both of the images and tell them what you want. It will probably cost you less than $50, so you have no excuse. If you cannot do it yourself, exercise your leadership qualities and hire someone to do it for you.

Sighting Your Scope | Who Is Your Customer?

Once you have determined what you do, decide who your customer (or target market) is. This may seem like it will be easy if you are doing success planning for a family, but don't skip it. What if extended family will be involved? What about a significant other?

So who is your customer? Many businesses and organizations will say "anyone," but that is rarely, if ever, true. It's time to erase the words someone, anyone and everyone from your vocabulary when it comes to your target market.

> *A gentleman at a networking meeting who was in the skin care industry said his target market was a person who had skin. That sounds true, and a bit humorous, on the surface, but it is actually not accurate. A newborn child in Iceland probably is not his target market.*

When you think of the word customer, most people think of the person who is going to purchase your product or service. But the target audience of your strategic vision (from the last section) may also be employees, vendors, family members, and the spouses of those people. If that is the case, those people are also your customer.

\ \ \

Daniel heads the HR department of a county government. The county is considered large, within the top 50 of the largest county populations in the United States, so this government agency is pretty big. The HR department alone consists of 42 employees.

Daniel has gathered the top-level managers of the department for a vision planning session. They are discussing how they can best serve their customer, the employees of the government agency, in the next five years. Part of their strategy is figuring out how to best utilize staff for maximum effectiveness. But they forgot that their staff is also part of their target market.

\ \ \

The preceding scenario shows how important it is to create and pinpoint your target market. Is your market mostly male or female? Don't say both. This is your *target* market, the low-hanging fruit of your customer base. These are the people that will be most likely to purchase your product or use your service.

There are three basic markets, and only two that you would want to look at:

1. Target market is your low hanging fruit. This is the type of person that is most likely to purchase your product or service.

2. Secondary market is the next likely type of customer; or marketing to your target out of season.

3. Tertiary market is the rest of the world. Usually only very large corporations use tertiary marketing.

To determine your target market, answer the following:

- Under what age group do they fall?

- What is their ethnicity?

- Where do they work?
- In what city do they live?
- Do they live in a house or apartment?
- What is their family life like?
- What is the average income?
- What kind of car do they drive?
- What are their goals?
- Where online do they go?
- Where are they most likely to hang out?
- What social media sites are they most likely to visit?
- What time of day do they visit?

You can put your target market on the head of a pin if you answer these questions, but don't stop with them. Figure out more questions to ask about your potential customers. The more you know your target market, the more successful you are likely to be.

This exercise is just as important if you are a business delivering a product or service, a leader building a team, a church building a ministry, or a family.

You may ask why these questions are important, especially goals. Why do you care what your target market's goals are? A person who sells sports cars for a living probably would not have a large target market at a tractor pull. The goals of people that attend tractor pulls may not generally include wanting an import sports car.

So how much money could be wasted if that person did a lot of advertising during a tractor pull? That's not to say it would not be worth advertising there, but determining your target market will help you to know how effective it may be.

There are other considerations as well. What is the culture, or tribe, of your target customer? Are you able to communicate with them on a level that will work for them? It would be difficult for a college professor to be told she needs to give a lecture to a 5th grade class the next day if she has never done so before. Likewise, a professional plumber may have a tough time giving a speech on the intricacies of pipe materials to auto mechanics.

What does your target customer need? What do they want? Is the problem you are solving *high* on their list? When will they buy? You see car ads during the Christmas season because people, historically, rarely buy cars during the holidays and the car companies want to change that; but that is secondary marketing. Clothing stores do not advertise swim suits in January or big down coats in July. Are you trying to sell ice to an Eskimo?

How will your target market perceive the price? If you have an amazing widget that you are selling for fifty cents each and you are marketing to Fortune 500 CEOs, you may not actually sell many of your items. This market may wonder how good the item is if it only costs fifty cents. Likewise, the target market for a luxury time-share may not be people living below the poverty level.

But what if your target market has nothing to do with buying a product or service? What if your customer is a member of a volunteer ministry in a church? It actually does not matter. Whether you are selling a product or service, promoting a new non-profit organization, or setting up a small group ministry, your vision is to provide a solution to a need that people want.

Explaining the intricacies of how the Biblical Old Testament and New Testament fit together to create a compelling story could drive a bunch of 3 year-olds to start throwing their toys; so those children would not be a good target market for that type of service.

Competitors

Who is your competitor and how do they engage with their target market? Who are they going after, and why? I have seen organizations going after the most unlikely of clients.

A local hardware store put an advertisement in a Christmas circular designed to engage women because they were offered a good price on the ad. But, chances are, that ad did little or nothing for them because the ad was about tools. They didn't advertise items that that generally appeal to that particular market. Had the ad been about Christmas plants or something similar, it may have done much better.

Look at where your competition is advertising and who they are marketing to. Is that a market you want to go after? Is it a low-hanging fruit (target) market, or a secondary market like the car companies do over the holidays? What makes that market compelling to your competition? Are they crazy, or is there an aspect that you may have not yet recognized?

Take a close look at your target market and answer the questions in this section. Many people skip this over, thinking that they know who their target market is. But 85% of businesses fail also.[9] If you want to rise above the statistics, you need to do the work that others are not willing to do.

Your Game Plan | How Are You Going To Do It?

Game plan sounds a little more exciting than strategy to me. Strategy brings to mind sitting around looking at a big map; while game plan seems more action oriented. I also like game plan because we're talking about the big game. Yes we're planning for success; and success is the big game. This is where the rubber meets the road. It's where you're going to work on the action steps for your success plan.

Think of your vision. How are you going to get from where you are now to where your vision is? Who is going to help you? What is the first step? Where are the most likely places obstacles will pop up? These are just some of the questions that should be answered when you develop your game plan.

You don't need to change some of the five success planning steps. Your why, your core values and your edict (or mission), don't need to change once you set them up. They can change if you want, but those steps don't have to; and I would recommend not altering them once they're done unless there is a compelling reason to make those changes.

Some items do change. Your vision should have an end date. Once your vision is done, it is a reality and time to start a new vision (you can keep your why, core values and edict even if you change the vision). There are books and articles that talk about visions that don't have end dates, but like I said in the strategic vision section, I believe a vision without an end date is nothing more than a dream.

Your target market can change and, if you have multiple products or services, you should have several target markets. Your target market for one item may not be the same as another item. And you may need to change your target market if something is not selling like it should.

Your game plan should be like an ocean, constantly changing and completely fluid. It's going to change a lot as time goes on. Everything you do should be part of the game plan, but it doesn't have to be part of the original plan.

Think about a volleyball game. While each volleyball team has 4-6 players, they switch positions each time they win a serve. And, although each team member has a specific spot that they start in, once that ball gets hit all heck can break loose. Everybody is everywhere. The players sometimes try to get back to their positions, but it all depends on where that ball goes.

That's how your game plan should be. Starting out it will be exactly what you want, but you need to change it as things happen. Preparing the steps of your game plan will make it a lot smoother as changes happen. And document changes to the plan.

Sometimes in the day to day grind we lose sight of the vision. However, if you document changes to the game plan you can see where you started your off-road journey and it will be easier to get back on track.

Your game plan is the process of executing the edict and the strategic vision that you have already devised and is going to tell you how you accomplish that edict and vision. It answers the questions of how and who. It is important because it is the final step in determining if the vision is realistic, as well as designing the steps to accomplish the vision.

In the section on determining your strategic vision, one of the steps is to figure out if that vision is realistic. It can be easy to flub that step due to the excitement you have for seeing that vision come to life. But it is more difficult to gloss that over here. Sometimes we have a vision that turns out to be unrealistic once the steps to achieve it are written down.

Your game plan determines if the vision is realistic within the timeline you decided upon. It details the process to accomplish that vision and it creates buy-in because most game plans are not carried out by an individual.

It doesn't matter if you are a solopreneur or you are determining your personal game plan for your future. The fact is almost no game plan can be accomplished without the help of other people. You might have family or friends that will help you, freelancers, contractors and strangers you will need to talk to about specialties. There is a small possibility it could just be you, but chances are you will not be able to accomplish it alone.

> ***Do you currently have a game plan? If you just gave me a blank stare, you may be following someone else's game plan. And, if***

you are following someone else's game plan, you are working toward their vision.

Maybe it's time to start on your own success plan, but it does not have to be independent of the success plan of the company where you work. You can create your vision and game plan to be in sync with the game plan of the company or organization you work for.

But now, rather than just working to make them successful, you can work to make yourself more successful at the same time.

Questions to Ask

Your game plan is similar to your vision in some respects: It focuses on what will be. It is a good idea to start with the end in mind; start with where your vision is. What is your vision? What does it look like? Now work your way backwards. I'll go through the steps here in just a bit.

What is your current game plan? Is it detailed, or are you living day to day and going where the wind blows you? We all have a game plan that we're working toward, but is it detailed enough that you are constantly working toward your vision? Add some detail to your current plan by looking at these three things:

- What's working in that plan?
- What's not working?
- What needs to be changed?

But you will probably need to develop a new game plan. Chances are you're reading this section because your current game plan is not working correctly. It is probably not in line with your vision, edict, core values, and your why.

In fact, could I hazard to say that you have an idea of a vision and a rough game plan, but the other three haven't been thought of yet. Don't kick yourself if that is true. This is not the time for a pity party; it's time for a success party because you are now on the road to success. Besides, pity parties are not fun and nobody brings presents.

The goal for your game plan is the successful completion of your strategic vision. When your game plan ends; your vision should be accomplished.

- What specifically do you need to do to accomplish that vision?
- Who is going to be involved?
- Who are the decision makers?
- Who will be the workers?
- What is your role in accomplishing the vision? Will you be the stakeholder, the facilitator, a worker, or is your job just to create the paperwork?

Write down each of these questions and answer them one at a time.

> *Take a closer look if you think you will be the only person working toward your vision. There is a small chance it will be only you, but it is more likely that you will need the help of other people. And there are sometimes problems when working with other people.*

This is an obstacle that introverted leaders need to overcome. We would prefer to complete our visions ourselves, but that is rarely possible. So be sure to list that as an obstacle as well as ways to overcome it.

What assets are needed to accomplish this game plan? What will it cost? This is a question many entrepreneurs don't ask and it is a very important question: What will the game plan cost? Where will the money come from? What if it doesn't come from there? What options do you have?

Where will it take place? Will it take place where you are now or will you need a new facility? Maybe you don't have a facility and you'll need your first facility. What obstacles need to be overcome as far as working space?

These are all important questions in determining your game plan. Not all the questions will apply to you; and there may be questions you need to ask that are not listed, but this should be a good start.

Designing Your Game Plan

Take another look at your strategic vision. What are some major milestones you can think of on the path to seeing your vision as a reality? Make a list of every milestone you can think of that you need to accomplish.

Jennifer's strategic vision is a promotion at work, but where she wants to be is two steps above where she is now. She has noticed that most the people that get promotions have college degrees, but she does not currently have one. Some milestones in her game plan could be:

- Have a conversation with my boss about my career goals, get advice.
- Sign up for an appropriate college program.
- Graduate from college
- Work toward the next promotion opportunity.

and on.

"Generate Small Wins" – Kouzes & Posner[10]

Write down all of your milestones, and then prioritize. What is the first milestone? Then ask what the first action step for that milestone might be. What is the first thing you can do right now to help you get one step closer to that milestone?

Write down each action step, starting with the first, that you will need to accomplish in order to get to that first milestone. Then go to the next milestone and start writing down all the action steps for that one, and so on.

What assets will you need to accomplish the vision? Are they currently available, or will they come from somewhere else? Will you need to talk to other organizations in order to get the assets, or will you need to buy them? What will the assets cost? Is there a certain quality that will be needed from some of the assets?

\ \ \

As an example, I watched a movie not too long ago. I won't say the name of the movie, but it was excellent. The actors did an amazing job and the way that the actors interacted with each other was compelling. The plot was very good as well.

But the music was terrible. The score was sub-par and the songs they chose did not fit with the movie at all. The movie was rated two and a half stars with several hundred ratings. I have no doubt it was because the music didn't fit with everything else.

If the right people would have composed the score and the right kind of music picked, it could easily have been a four or five star movie. A movie score is an asset. Find the right asset and find the right people that have the assets.

\` \` \`

And this is the point where 90% of the rest of the people stop success planning: Money. There, the word is out there. But don't stop here. Money isn't everything, but it can help make things happen. And, unless you are leading a group of volunteers, employees generally like to get paid; so your game plan needs to include a budget.

But don't worry about how high the figures get when you first design your game plan. Go wild when you first write it out. Pare the numbers down later if you need to, but don't limit yourself at first. Detail what it will cost.

How much will it take to hire the needed people? What's the cost of the assets? What are the running costs? What, financially, will it take to accomplish this game plan?

The cost isn't just money. How much time will it take? Will you need contractors, and what will their hourly wage be? If you plan on using volunteers, where will you find them? How many hours do you need from the volunteers? Will you use interns? What will their hourly wage be?

Then ask what costs are you not considering? It can be easy to overlook certain things if we don't think about that. Is there another group or organization that has done something similar? Can you get a copy of their budget? Can you contact them and ask what unexpected things happened on their journey? That could help you see areas you may have missed. It may also be a good idea to add in an extra 10% (or an amount you are comfortable with) to account for the unexpected.

Did the number you came up with surprise you? Are you wondering where all that money will come from? Are you starting to think the end date of your vision was too ambitious? Make needed changes to the success plan before you start, but don't make those changes just yet.

Get the team together (if there is one) for a planning session after you have all the numbers together. Look everything over to figure out if anything is missing and where money can be saved. Costs might be allocated in one area that aren't needed in that area, but they may be needed in another area. Can you move them?

There are some organizations where certain departments have more money than they need and other departments have less than they need; but they can't move money between departments.

Where can money be saved? Can you design your game plan so money that is being made in one area can be spent on another area? Are there things you can do on the side to make the needed money? The cost of the game plan should include options on how the money will come in.

\ \ \

Joe owned a construction company and recently got awarded the biggest contract he had ever had; a 30-house subdivision. He was to be paid an equal amount after a certain number of houses were completed, but that meant he needed working capital in between each phase of the project.

He soon found out that the permitting process sometimes took a week or two, so he would have his crew doing smaller jobs for other companies during those times. This kept his crew working and allowed him to raise the capital he needed until the first big paycheck came in.

\` \` \`

Who will be involved? What positions need to be filled? Do you have the money to hire new employees and contractors (who sometimes ask for a certain amount up front)? You may be able to make a lot of money in the end, but do you have the money to pay them until the end?

What will need to be done to overcome those obstacles and can any be headed off right now? One obstacle could be personality differences. Why not have everybody on the team take a personality test so you can make sure the personalities are complimentary to each other?

Another option would be to hire a (business) team coach to help the group work better with each other. Of course, money would need to be allocated for that as well.

Your game plan is the action that comes out of your other four success planning items. Your game plan will be determined by your why and it will be influenced by your core values. Your edict will help you remember what you are doing, and when your vision becomes reality your game plan will be completed.

So, you have to make sure that your game plan is in line with each and every one of the other success planning items as you create each step.

The Getaway

Now that you have read through the first six sections on Success Planning, it's time to put your ideas to practice.

The Getaway is designed to be completed in four sessions, each consisting of about four hours. I recommend you do this over a two-day period.

Success planning is all about consistency, and consistently working on the plan is more beneficial because you don't have to retrain your brain at the start of each session. It takes time to get out of "working in" your business mode and getting into "working on" your business mode.

However, you can schedule each session on a different day if that works better for you. Maybe you can't get two consecutive days away, and you need to schedule four half-day sessions over the month. That's okay. Or maybe you want to take more time away and schedule once session per day over four days.

It's more important to *do it* than to not do it because you can't get exactly two days in a row. But if you schedule different days that are not consecutive, plan on time at the beginning of each session to shed the clutter in your mind.

The sessions can be just you, a team of people, or a family getaway. Try to get everyone who has a stake in the plan to be there, but don't invite friends or people that will take your mind off your task.

Plan a weekend away if you can. If you cannot, try to find a place away from both work and home for each session. Many hotels have conference rooms that can be rented by the day. If that is not feasible, maybe a park or a coffee shop would work.

Pick a place where you will be comfortable and have access to everything you need. And try to schedule fun time in the middle of each session or a time to stop and enjoy peace and quiet.

My favorite place for success planning is a hotel by the ocean during winter. There is a conference room for everyone to gather and internet access for live streaming. In between sessions, I love to take private walks on the beach to help my mind relax and unwind between sessions.

However, I have also found success working in busy coffee shops (but this is best for a group of 1-3. Any more and it becomes difficult to hear). The other customers are so caught up in what they are doing that we get completely ignored. And, I get the added benefit of people-watching.

Find a space where your creativity can flow, but make sure it is a space that will allow you to be there for up to four hours without disturbing anyone. More importantly, make sure it's a place you won't be disturbed much.

A restaurant will have waiters or waitresses coming to ask if you need anything (and finding polite ways to get you to leave so they can help another customer). Coffee shops, however, rarely have wait staff walking around.

Take a good break between each session if you are doing multiple sessions each day. Go get something to eat, take in the local sites, but DO NOT do work. Stay away from working IN as much as possible. This is a time for working ON.

If your mind gets too cluttered with other tasks that need to be done, write them down so you can get back to them later. The act of writing them down allows your brain to be free of having to remember the tasks.

In The Beginning

The four sessions should ideally be done over a two-day period. We are so used to working IN our lives, in the day-to-day grind, that we need time to get out of "work mode." If possible, get off work the day before and start shedding that work mode.

Relax, watch a movie or read a book. Spend time with close friends, but stay away from big, loud parties. That will shut down your introverted mind all too quickly.

Working ON your life, business, career, ministry, etc. takes a lot of mental energy and there are some things you can do to help your brain be prepared for the day ahead.

Eat healthy: It is tempting to eat junk food during the getaway (at least it is for me). However, junk food is going to give you a short high then a crash. Eat vegetables and lean meat. Try to stay away from high carb and high fat foods.

Are you old enough to remember the "this is your brain on drugs" commercials with the fried egg? If not, look it up on the internet. That is just one of the fun commercials we were subjected to when I was younger. But it makes a good point.

Your body and your brain both need the right kind of energy for optimal output. Working ON you takes brain power, so feed your brain correctly for this exercise.

Be prepared: Make sure you have everything you need for the session. If you are working on your strategy, do you have your written why, core values, edict and vision handy? Get your laptop, tablet, pad of paper and pens, healthy snacks (I like protein or nut bars), and whatever else you need.

Make sure you have a large screen TV or whiteboard if you are working in a group. You don't want to be scrambling for things in the middle of planning; it could make for a chaotic and unproductive session. See Appendix 4 for a sample checklist of things to bring.

Pick the place according to the people attending: List the people involved if this is a group effort. How many extroverts (if you don't know, ask) will be attending? The place you pick will be different if you have all introverts or if you were brave enough to invite extroverts along (a good idea, by the way. They think different from introverts and can contribute a lot. Don't go there, YES, they can too contribute. Test your leadership skills by limiting their talking). Even if you are alone, pick the place carefully.

That doesn't mean you have to find a log cabin that is a 10-hour hike away from the nearest road. The Las Vegas strip can be a good place as long as where you will be doing the work is comfortable for you.

I used to do some great writing in the middle of Pike Place Market in Seattle. The market is a sea of people in the summer, but there were so many people that nobody paid me any attention at all. And, the constant buzz allowed me to concentrate on what I was doing.

It did, however, still overwhelm me after a couple of hours. A good idea would be to have a quiet place that is close by to go to when that happens.

Now I do my best work either when completely alone in my office or in a coffee shop that is not too busy. And my getaways are usually quiet hotels near the ocean. I video conference when I need to bring others in. I do, however, like to pick tourist towns so I can get out of the room and find fun things to do between sessions.

Again, that also depends on the people. A cabin in the mountains may sound like heaven to you, but it will drive extroverts batty (don't get any ideas; I am not advocating the extinction of extroverts). Finding just the right place for everyone may be a bit challenging, but it will be worth it.

Be Mindful: Get in the right frame of mind for each session. Try this before you start:

15 minutes to tranquility:

Take 15 minutes and work some positive expectation in your mind.

- Spend the first 5 minutes on what you are grateful for. Think of all the positive things that are going on in your life now. See them in your mind. Remember past successes. Failures may try to creep themselves into the picture, ignore them. Or, if that doesn't work, try imagining a file cabinet and, whenever a negative thought comes forward; file it away in the cabinet. Write down your positive experiences if that will help.
- Take 5 minutes to pray or meditate. Control your breathing during this time. Nice, slow, steady, deep breaths. Do not hold your breath or breathe shallowly. The body and the brain love oxygen, give them both plenty of it.
- Take the last 5 minutes and envision the session ahead. Imagine having already

accomplished it. Think of how you will feel when it is completed.

The Sessions

This is how I recommend doing the sessions. Feel free to change it if something else works better for you, but I have found this to be quite productive:

- Session 1: Why and Core Values
- Session 2: Mission and Edict
- Session 3: Strategic Vision and Target Market
- Session 4: Game Plan

Do two sessions a day if you are planning a weekend getaway. I picked 4-hour sessions on purpose. Not all four hours are supposed to be concentrating on planning.

I would recommend the first 15 minutes be spent alone, each person doing the 15 minutes to tranquility. Once that is done, eat together if it is a group. This is all part of your first 4-hour session. You might start brainstorming while you eat or you might not, either way is okay.

Designate one person as the official note taker even if everyone will be writing things down. If you are alone, remember to write everything down or record your session. Get a whiteboard or an easel pad (maybe both). If you are a techy-nerd, try to have at least one of the laptops hooked to a big screen TV.

Take a break about halfway through each session. Four hours is a long time (even for introverts) to concentrate on success planning. Get out of the room for a bit, change coffee shops, whatever it takes to break the cycle for a while.

> ***Ever notice that the solution to a problem sometimes comes when you are doing something completely different? Maybe you are stuck on figuring something out, so you get away for a bit and go mow the lawn or get your nails done.***
>
> ***Then, halfway through your new project the solution hits you. Remember to finish your new project, though; having your nails half-done or the lawnmower in the***

middle of a half-finished lawn would look weird.

Now, if your session gets finished before the four hours is up, fantastic! Take that extra time and go have fun. Watch a show, relax on the balcony, or take the dogs to the dog park. Part of the reason to schedule four hours is to schedule relaxing time. Success planning is mentally stressful; give your brain a chance to unwind between sessions and at the end of the day.

Party time! Last, but not least, when you are done, have a party! But party the introvert way. First (most definitely first), send the extroverts to a social party. They will thank you. Politely (yes, politely) decline their invitation to join them. If they say extroverty things like "but it will be fun," agree with them. Reply with "I'm glad you will have fun. I am going to have fun my way."

Then each introvert should go to their own quiet place for at least an hour to recharge. If you want to get back together to eat or go to a movie after that, do it. But don't feel guilty if you want to spend the rest of the night completely alone. The other introverts will probably feel the same, and the extroverts won't even think about you once they get to small talking with complete strangers.

Finally, remember to keep what you did safe. Refer to it often. You've just wasted a lot of brain power and time if you don't. Print out your vision and edict and frame them. Put them on your web site or office wall. Keep your game plan on your desk and refer to it whenever you are not sure of what you should be doing.

Be proud of what you did, it was a lot of work!

Chapter 5 ~ Ambivert Leadership

Jim Collins, in his book *Good to Great,*[1] writes about making sure to get the right people on the bus (and the wrong people off the bus). But he doesn't talk about the bus. The "bus" is your Why and your vision for the future.

Most corporate visions, up to this point, have been created by extroverts (you can tell by words like *us, team,* and *together).* As an introvert leader you have the opportunity to level the playing field, to create an ambivert way to lead.

Yes, it is tempting to create an introverted document but the extroverts will revolt, and revolting extroverts are not fun; they are louder than happy extroverts.

Leading Extroverts

Unless you are a hermit, you have some extrovert qualities. And hermits are not leaders so I doubt any hermits are reading this book. You have probably pretended to be an extrovert in the past, so their personality and skills are not as foreign to you as your skills are to them (I have never known an extrovert try to pretend to be an introvert). And there are certain things you have probably learned to expect when encountering extroverts in the concrete jungle.

Extroverts can be loud and obnoxious. They tend to speak without first thinking; they have the absurd idea that nothing can be done unless it is by committee, and... life would be nowhere near as fun without them. However, no matter what you think of them, you cannot be a good leader without working with and understanding extroverts.

Not tolerating, understanding. Yes, for a long time introverts were thought to be less adaptable than extroverts. In fact, not so long ago the American Psychiatric Association tried to categorize introversion as a mental health issue.[2] But those days are gone and it doesn't matter what they think of us, we can overcome that by being great leaders.

A great leader works at understanding those he/she leads. Extroverts like to talk, so talk to them. But plan out what you are going to say. This will help both them and you. When you have a plan it will give them less of a chance to change the subject and talk about the weather, their dog, the color of the carpet, the weather again, and such.

Look at how the extroverts like to interact and find ways that you can incorporate introversion into the interaction. Do not try to take over their way of doing things, find common ground that you can both stand upon.

And remember, there are some extroverts that have a habit of putting us down and throwing little jabs our way; do not copy them (however, they may need a verbal or written warning if they are trying to undermine your leadership).

Use your strengths during difficult situations. Exercise your introverted leadership skills to set up a training session for extroverts on how to best interact with introverts. Make it a fun exercise, maybe even using some comedy to show drastic differences between extroverts and introverts. Knowledge is power; your team will grow in confidence quicker when they know how to work well with each other.

"Psychologists tell us that one of the most powerful forces in humanity is acceptance. It's what we all crave."[3]

And keep it fair; go the other direction as well. Find a good extrovert and have them create a training session on how introverts can better interact with extroverts. A good leader will accept his/her limitations and work to grow his/her strengths.

Leaders need to develop a thick skin and help those they lead to do the same. You need your people to know that you have their back. Ask questions like: "You seemed a bit on edge earlier; is there anything I can help with?" Or "would you like to talk about it?" And be consistent; your people will begin to respect you when they know you aren't just throwing words around, but that you really mean what you say.

Don't be afraid to ask your team questions about how they are doing. But don't swap stories. For instance, an extrovert may have been having an argument with their kid. Your first reaction may be to tell them how you handled a similar situation, but watch out for that. Some people see what you are saying as a shared experience. Others, however, may think that you are trying to show that you are better than they are because you handled the situation a different way.

So try to keep comments to yourself and let them talk. Listen actively by nodding at what they say and asking specific questions about the situation. In other words, use the introvert skills you have to help extroverts.

Team Communication

What does your boss want? What do those who work under you want? Are you sure, or are you making an assumption? Introverts are good at assuming that other people misunderstand them. However, because of their quiet nature, introverts do not generally correct those assumptions. This is as true of those you lead as it is of you.

Introvert leaders need to communicate well and establish expectations for the team; the team will fail without proper expectations being communicated. There is a common saying that everything rises and falls on leadership, and that may be true. However, if it is, then communication is one of the tools that will either allow a leader to rise or cause them to fall. Introvert leaders need to find effective ways to communicate with their team that also works with their personality.

This does not mean a round-robin team meeting or a group video session. Email may be better for establishing expectations, but crafting a proper email may require help. We introverts generally love the economy of words. However, using fewer words sometimes creates the illusion of a stern message.

Important team emails may need the help of an extrovert. So the next time you write a team email, send it to an extroverted member of the team or a colleague and ask their opinion on how it reads. You may need to add "fluffy" words to the email so it does not come across like you are angry or upset.

And don't be afraid to text or leave a note on a desk. We are introverts, why waste time talking?

Meetings

Meetings are the playground of extroverts. Meetings are where they can shine, happily exchanging handshakes and talking about... nothing important whatsoever. But they do it with such passion! True, good things come out of meetings, but they are not tailored for introverts. In fact, meetings have the tendency to make introverts shut down from over stimulation.

There are ways, however, to help introverts during meetings.

- The meeting leader can send out the agenda a day or two in advance. This will give introverts time to see what the topics are and develop a conversation plan.
- Participants can be encouraged to provide input later. Give the introverts in the group time to process. Yes, the extroverts may come up with ideas quickly, but before the leader puts his/her stamp of approval on it, give the quieter people time to submit their ideas. Remember, important things are rarely urgent and urgent things are rarely important.

Creative meetings are, by their very nature, self-limiting. Have you ever noticed that once one person comes up with an idea, everyone gets around it and refines it rather than coming up with more new ideas?

One way to alleviate that is to have everyone submit ideas before the meeting. Then, at the meeting, display all the ideas that everyone came up with (without names so nobody feels embarrassed) so the group can discuss them. And again, allow everyone time after the meeting for further input before a decision is made.

Team Building for Introverts

Example of an extrovert and introvert who are forced to work together but have no respect or rapport for each other.
Extrovert: "You are the expert in computer problems, what is wrong with this computer?"

Introvert: Sits quietly looking at the computer, not saying anything.

Extrovert: "Talk to me, what is wrong with the computer?"

Introvert: "Not sure." Then he starts tinkering with the computer. But he is flustered because the extrovert is standing over him and won't stop talking long enough for him to concentrate.

Extrovert: "Well, if you can't fix it, I'll call someone who can." He is now frustrated because, from what he can tell, the introvert is not fixing the problem and not talking to him about what the problem may be.

They both want the same thing; to fix the problem. However, they each have different ways of communicating and neither one of them is willing to try to meet in the middle.

Remember, you need to get people involved, so make a list of who that will be. What does the team look like? What do the personalities on that team look like? What kind of people do you envision being there? How are you going to work with the people?

According to Meyers-Briggs, there are 16 basic personality types.[4] Figure out what personality types would work best on your team. Are you a visionary (common in leaders)? Are you dependable, practical? What other personality traits do you have? If you don't know, find out.

There are many personality type indicators, take several of them.[5] Write your personality traits down and determine where your strengths and weaknesses are.

Leaders with low self-confidence will tend to gather people with the same personality traits they have. If this is you, first, congratulations! I mean that. You are admitting that you have a weakness, and that is a great step in leadership. I highly recommend that you engage with a professional coach so you can better understand where that comes from. However, at the same time, try to pick people for your team that are completely opposite from you. Proper teams are made up of people that are not afraid to stand up to the leader when needed.

> *We all want to work alongside people that we get along with, but the best team is made of different personality types. The*

introvert leader could benefit a great deal by having an extrovert right-hand person.

Are there currently people in the organization that would fit on your team; or will you need new people? What will the cost be of those new people? What kind of personality will those people need to have?

Your Why and Core Values (from Chapter 4) will help you pick your team. Make sure their core values align with yours. Dysfunctional teams start with mismatched core values.

You may have already determined your edict and strategic vision, but your team needs to own these as well. Once your team is in place, bring your edict and strategic vision to them and ask them what needs to be changed. Do not ask them to buy off on what you did, let them decide for themselves.

"Not finance. Not strategy. Not technology. It is teamwork that remains the ultimate competitive advantage, both because it is so powerful and so rare"
– Patrick Lencioni[6]

5 Stages of Team Development

Dr. Bruce Tuckman published his book on the 5 stages of team development in 1965 and these stages still apply today. They are:

Forming: It is critical to bring in the right personalities for a team. A successful team will be made up of people that have similar core values, as described above.

\`\`\`

Jim is an excellent programmer, one of the best in the company. He has been invited to join the Artificial Intelligence team that is doing ground-breaking work. Jim is excited to be a part of such a prestigious group.

However, within a few days of being on the team Jim realizes that the entire purpose of the team is to create better advertising algorithms for the 1-5 year old market. Jim decides to look into it further and realizes that this group is trying to figure out how properly manipulate advertising so young children will grow up wanting a certain product.

\`\`\`

This goes completely against Jim's core values and, as a result, Jim will not be a good fit for that team.

Many companies do not think about individual core values when putting teams together. But, similar core values are critical to proper team formation.

Storming: This is the time when personalities clash. Everyone got together to do something, but everyone wants it done a different way.

\ \ \

You've all heard of Des. Des joined the US Army as a medic during World War II. He refused to pick up or fire a rifle during basic training, and was almost thrown out. The US Military determined that Des had core values different from theirs.

Despite a difficult time in basic training, he got through and was assigned to 2nd Platoon, B Company where he again refused to pick up or fire a rifle.

But Des, Corporal Desmond Doss, was a medic. He received two Bronze Stars in 1944 for ". . .exceptional valor in aiding wounded soldiers under fire,"[7] and eventually became the only conscientious objector to ever earn the Medal of Honor.

\ \ \

Many people assumed Corporal Doss had a certain set of core values because of a certain action (refusing to pick up a gun). The truth is that he had the exact core values needed of a military medic during war time.

The movie *Hacksaw Ridge* portrays a dramatic showing of how Corporal Doss was treated before he saved his fellow Army soldiers. It is a perfect example of storming.

Many volunteer teams will break up at this stage. Leaders need to do a lot of listening and communicating here to keep the team together.

Norming: Developing a shared edict and strategic vision is critical for a team to start norming. It is the backbone the team can get behind.

But the edict and vision are just the beginning. Norming is when the team settles down and starts seeing, with more clarity, the similarities each of them have. Individuals have begun to function better together as a team and start forming relationships that clear a path toward objectives.

This is where people start to let their guard down and begin to trust each other more. It is also where leaders need to watch team dynamics and check for the forming of inner groups, or cliques. A clique can destroy a team before the leader knows what‘s going on, so watch carefully for how relationships are developing.

Performing: Relationships between team members are doing well and there are few personality flare-ups at this stage. If you think of the shoe-tying analogy in the Competence section of Chapter 3, this would be the “conscious competent” stage. Everyone knows what to do, but they still need to concentrate on the task.

Leaders can use this stage to help the team get better at what they do and to help members rely on each other. There is more trust in the group, so it is easier for individuals to talk about their weaknesses and get help.

Many teams do not reach this stage because there is a lack of trust in the organization as a whole. It is difficult for a person to trust a team when the organization lacks trust, but a leader can prove to the team that he/she is trustworthy by having their backs.

Have you noticed that "team building" and being a "team player" is so important in today's corporate world? But, the higher you get, the less of a team player you are. How many teams is the average CEO a part of?

Transforming: The perfect team is a well-oiled machine and needs little leadership. The transforming stage is where the leader almost becomes just another team member. Everyone is doing their job so well that they don't need much direction.

This is the stage that every corporation strives for in their teams, but many corporate executives try to bypass the steps before this one. It does not work, of course. There is no way to develop a new team and have it start at the transforming stage, even if every member already knows and trusts one another.

The Team Player

Alone we can do so little; together we can do so much - Helen Keller

Even leaders need to be team players. Remember when you were a kid and your parents made you share your toys with the other kids? Then you grew up and found out that adults don't share toys (so stop asking that friend with the Lamborghini). Instead, adults are supposed to be team players. How extroverty.

But leaders cannot expect others to be team players without being one themselves. And since the role of a leader is to support their team, he/she must be the lead team player. Luckily, it's not as difficult as it sounds. Here are some tips on how to be both a good leader and team player.

Active Listening

One of the key responsibilities of a team player also happens to be one of the best things introverts do: Active listening. Every conversation between two or more people involves talking and listening (If only one person is talking it's called a speech, not a conversation). However, active listening is not a skill that many people have. Most people will be thinking of what they are going to say next rather than intently listening to what the other person is saying.

\`\`\`

I went to a networking meeting one day, but I should not have been there. It had been a stressful morning and I had a lot going on in my mind. I was not paying much attention to my surroundings while talking to a nice lady when she suddenly asked me if I did something to upset her.

I snapped back to the present and replied no, not at all. She mentioned that I had rolled my eyes, to which I apologized and felt terrible about. But the damage was done, I never saw her again.

\`\`\`

That is a good example of what active listening is not. It doesn't matter if you're an introvert or an extrovert; it pays to be present during conversations.

Active listening is a lot more than just paying attention to the conversation. This is a great skill for introverts to practice; especially since we are natural listeners. Active listening includes affirmative responses.

For instance, saying things like "good point," "yeah," or even "uh-huh" shows that you are not just hearing what the other person is saying; but that you are actually listening and understanding their part of the conversation. But the best way to show active listening is to say back what the person said to you in different words. For instance:

John: "Leadership is influence."

Mary: "So if you influence people, you are a leader?"

Leaders need to go beyond active listening, however. Being a leader and a team player means that you need to be serious about the ideas others have and do one of two things:

1. Act on the idea. Do not hesitate to act on a great idea a fellow team member may have. This will accomplish two things; first, it lets the other person know that you respect and value their thoughts. Second, it lets the rest of the team know this okay to come up with ideas.
2. Let the team member know that you are not going to act on that idea and why. Be respectful. Introverts have a way of minimizing words and sometimes it can

make others think that you do not value them (it is good to practice that conversation with a person you trust). You always want to make sure that your team member knows that you are glad they came up with an idea and, even though you are not going to use that particular idea, you want them to keep coming up with more.

Leading Events

Events are difficult, stressful, and exasperating. And they can be a great deal of fun at the same time. But don't try to do an event alone, especially if you are speaking. Find an extrovert that can be the greeter; someone who can talk to people before and during the event. The last thing you want to do is be social right before you go on stage; you could be exhausted before you even start.

Take time to be alone in a quiet place before you go on stage. Maybe get onto social media (not live) and make a couple of quick posts, go over your talking notes or just relax for a while.

Decide whether you want to answer some questions after you are done. If you do, schedule a Q&A section for the end of the presentation so you are not caught off-guard. If not, give the audience ways to contact you with questions. Introverts hate surprises so try to be prepared for everything you can.

Most importantly, be polite. It is difficult when you are drained after a presentation, but you can do it. If someone catches you in the hallway, be nice to them. One smart way to help the audience to prepare for this is to incorporate something about you being an introvert into the presentation. That way, they won't be as surprised if you disappear shortly after your presentation or speech is over.

Leadership Marketing For Introverts

Networking

Networking is almost a four-letter word to an introvert, but it is one of the things that leaders need to do. Part of a leader's job is to promote their team; whether it is in a meeting, at a social gathering, to a referral networking group, or to potential new members. Each of those situations calls for hand shaking and engaging in small talk to people you do not know well, or at all.

The thought of such an activity may sound very intimidating, but there are things you can do to prepare. If the purpose is to promote your team, what aspects do you want to promote? Plan ahead what you might say or create talking points and practice them.

Do you know anything about the other people that will be there? If not, can you look them up and do a bit of cyber-stalking? Maybe you can find a similar interest to talk about.

Is one of your team members an uber-extrovert? Bring that person along to help create smoother conversations, but don't bring along a talker that doesn't know how to shut up. That will not help.

Networking groups

Networking, at its core, is word of mouth advertising. It is a great option for small business people and entrepreneurs as well as group leaders. But you need to carefully pick the type of group you are going to join. Here are the main types of networking groups:

> *For Extroverts:*
> *That person you see at networking groups that looks out of place and never talks to anyone is not being arrogant; That is an introvert that could use some help. They don't know how to show it, but they would like for you to talk to them.*

Referral Networking: These groups get together on a consistent basis so the members can inform others of what they do and who is a good referral (target market).

There are national groups you can join for a fee, and most larger cities have independent groups that may ask for a small fee or are free. The larger national groups generally have much better structures in place. However, it would still be prudent to check out independent groups.

Most national referral groups only allow one business per industry, but that can be deceiving. Many of them make more money the more people who join, so you may see a commercial real estate agent next to a residential real estate agent. Or, there may be an auto insurance person next to a home insurance person even though most people have both policies at the same company.

Referral networking is one of the easier groups for introverts to join, and is a good option if you are an entrepreneur or small business owner. And, although the national groups are generally more expensive, they are usually a better option for introverts due to the structure. Independent groups can deteriorate into social groups (see below), which means they will soon be gone.

Here's a rule of thumb for networking events: One new honest to goodness networking relationship is worth ten fistfuls of business cards. Rush home afterward and kick back on your sofa. Susan Cain, Quiet.[8]

Professional Associations: Even though the implication is that all the members will be part of the same industry (automobile, real estate, etc.), that is not generally the case. Professional associations sometimes allow vendors to join. For instance, contractors may be allowed to join a real estate association or accountants might be invited to join an automobile association.

Regardless of that, professional associations get together for the purpose to impart information about their specific industry. So take care about joining this type of group unless you are a part of the industry or can give wisdom to others in that particular industry in some way.

Mastermind Groups: Mastermind groups are everywhere, but they can be hard to find. Most mastermind groups have a leader that charges a fee to be part of the group. No more than one person per industry is invited, and potential members are screened.

The members get together at regular intervals, and one person will talk about a business problem they are having. Then the entire group will work together to help solve the problem.

Some mastermind groups are continuous and some have a specific start and stop date. However, most mastermind groups are closed once the second session has started. Trust is a big factor in mastermind groups and having new people join in the middle does not generally work.

Mastermind groups are starting to pop up on internet social media sites. This can be a good option for introverts. You can login, read what is going on, and reply after you have had time to think about the issue.

Social Networking (or, Networking Without a Purpose): As the name implies, this type of group is the bane of an introvert. I recommend that this type of group be the last on your list to join, if you decide to join at all. Social networking groups are generally a free-for-all. They entail cocktails and snacks with an open forum to talk about whatever you like.

Community Service: Community service groups are all about the neighborhood. They are groups of like-minded people that want to improve the local area or have a national or international agenda. Referrals can be given and received in these types of groups, but the purpose is to give to the community (of course, the PR you get in return does not hurt).

Relationship networking

Relationship networking is networking with the purpose of building relationships. It is generally for small business owners, real estate agents, and people in multi-level marketing companies and it's a great way to help people understand what exactly it is that you do.

Relationship networking sounds like the bane of an introvert's life, but it is not. Relationship networking is actually easier than most other (face to face) types of networking because it involves talking with a purpose; and you have the opportunity to talk about your business, organization, ministry, club, etc.

Social networking involves going to a meeting, usually in the evenings, that has no real purpose. Everyone stands around for X hours and talks about . . . nothing important. THAT is the bane of an introvert's night.

Relationship networking, on the other hand, involves two or three people. Some call it a "one-to-one," or other similar names and it can be integrated into any of the other types of networking. It is a popular activity in referral networking groups and, if done right, it is where an introvert can shine. Here is an example of what I mean:

Shane and Jennifer get together for a one-to-one over coffee. They sit down, say hi, and do a very introductory small talk exchange. Then one of them has a certain amount of time (usually about 30 minutes) to talk about themselves and their business.

This is where you get to explain what you do, why you do it and, most importantly; who your target market is. I recommend ending your time with two specific things:

1. "A good referral for me is . . ." Tell them how they can best refer people to you. Do not sell to them, even if they are a possible client. The purpose of this relationship is to refer to each other.

2. "What can I do for you?" Remember, the number one way to be successful is to help enough other people with their problems, whether you make money from it or not. You are establishing trust by asking what you can do for them, and you will establish a lot more trust if you do it.

Listening is a skill that comes more naturally to introverts than extroverts. Hone this skill, it is invaluable.

One tip for relationship networking: Take notes. Write down the person's name and what they do, get contact information and so on. *Most importantly* write down their concerns. If you listen close enough you will hear them.

And the relationship networking super-secret: Find a way to help alleviate any concerns you may have overheard. Perhaps you caught on that they are not good at marketing. Send them a link to a marketing book that helped you or others you know. I

f they mentioned that they were late because of a leaky faucet, car problems, etc., email them later with people you know that can help. These people would probably be other one-to-ones you have had in the past; email them also so they know you are sending a referral.

As an introvert, you can excel at this type of networking.

Public Speaking

Hey, don't look at me like that. I did *not* say anything disparaging about your mother and I did not cuss, although I know it sounds like I did.

So go ahead, cringe. Make that face like you just ate {*insert disgusting food here*}. I know it scares the heebeejeebees out of you, it does to everyone. But you are oh so much more prepared to speak in public than extroverts, and here's why: Public speaking is the domain of the introvert.

Yes, you heard me right *public speaking is the domain of the introvert.* Remember, there is a difference between shy and introvert. It's time to shed the shy act and embrace your introvertedness (yes, I just made that up) because We Can OWN public speaking.

What is public speaking? What is it really? It is nothing more than giving a speech about a topic that you know well. We introverts like talking about topics that we know well.

Public speaking is not interactive. You are in front of an audience with an invisible barrier between you and them; and *they know it.* Q&A sessions are up to you. Audience participation is up to you. When you step out in front of others, it's *your* domain and you call the shots.

> ***For Introverts: Extroverts are generally natural interactive conversationalists, but speeches are foreign to them. They can do a***

speech, but introverts are more naturally created to talk in front of audiences.

Of course there is a fear to overcome, and I have talked about fear before. I also talked about joining groups like Toastmasters. But I am not talking about shoving you in front of a huge audience tomorrow unprepared.

\ \ \

The first group I spoke in front of was 10 teenagers. I spent two weeks preparing a 20-minute speech I already knew. And, when it was over, I couldn't remember a single word I'd said or how I did.

The speech was for a group of at-risk teens. When it was over, one young man came up to me and thanked me for what I had said; and that was all it took. I don't think of people being in their underwear, I don't even see a crowd anymore.

As I start to talk now, I scan all the "background" for one person that is looking at me and I lock eyes with them for a few seconds as I talk. Then I scan the group for the next individual that I am going to talk to. I don't talk to crowds, I talk to different individuals. They just happen to be in the same place at the same time.

\ \ \

You control what you are going to say, how you are going to say it, and who you are going to talk to when you are on that stage.

Think about it: In what other situation can you get in front of a bunch of people, say what you want to say without anyone else talking or interrupting, then leave without a single conversation and still be the star? If I have to interact socially, I prefer to be on a stage now.

Chapter 6 ~ The Introverted Parent Leader

Is Your Child An Introvert or Extrovert?

The day will come when you realize that your child is either an introvert or an extrovert. Or, if you can't tell, your child may be an ambivert.

Leading An Introverted Child

You may think that you are uniquely qualified to lead an introverted child, and you might be much better off than an extrovert would be. However, look at how you were raised; did you have introverted parents that tried to get you to do more extroverted activities? You may need to overcome the impulse to do the same things your parents did, so watch out.

Help your introverted child to learn when it is break time. Show them that the irritable feelings they start to experience are not all bad, it just means they need some alone time to recharge. Don't make this a punishment, just a time for them to have solitude with a comic, book, computer or whatever works for you and them. And make sure it is time when they can be undisturbed.

The same goes for homework. Your introverted child is much like you; he or she needs a lot of quiet time, and they do not get it at school. Help them design a space that will work for their needs: A bedroom with a desk may be a great idea.

Or, if they share a bedroom, see if you can find a small space for them to do homework where they will not be disturbed. But make sure it is a space they accept, not one that is imposed upon them.

By all means; if you have other children, teach them the importance of quiet time, especially if you have some children that are introverts and some that are extroverts. This can be a great lesson for guests as well.

\ \ \

Jonny and Troy were good friends. One night Jonny invited Troy over for a sleepover. Everything was going great; they were playing and having a wonderful time. Then suddenly Troy got upset and demanded to call his mom to come get him. Have you been there before? Troy was an introvert and his energy ran out. Unfortunately, Troy didn't know that all he needed was a bit of alone time then he would be ready to go again (But, then again, some adults don't know that either).

\ \ \

If you know a child that suddenly has a breakdown for no apparent reason or over-exaggerates a small incident, that may be an introvert who needs solitude. Tread lightly here if this is not your child; they may think that they are in trouble. Let them know that nothing is wrong, it just seems a good time for everyone to take a break.

Finding an excuse for quiet time is a sign of a good parent leader. But don't just send them to their room. Suggest they work on their building blocks, read a book, watch a television show or whatever will work for them to know that it is not a punishment.

Then, after a while (after you have also had a break), check on them to see how they are doing. Point it out if they are feeling better. Show them that taking a break is a good thing. And talk to them about signs that they need a break so they can start to learn for themselves.

Introverted children will instinctively crawl into their shell at times, but that is not always the case. Introverted children, just like adults, will find their voice when it is a subject they are passionate about. As introverts ourselves, the instinct is to find a reason to get them to stop talking, but that may not be healthy for them. Your children need to know that it's good to talk, and the best leaders are good listeners.

Encourage your children to talk. If the timing is not convenient for you, don't just say "not now" or tell them you will talk to them later. They may feel discouraged and it may make them think that what they have to say does not matter. Tell them you need to finish what you are doing (or finish your own introvert time) and will be able to talk in 10 minutes, an hour, or some specific time. And keep that time.

Leading a young child

First, forget about trying to lead an infant, just love on them. Infants couldn't care less about leadership. As long as they can eat, cry, and poop when they want (sometimes all at once), they are happy.

Leading a younger child (ages 4-8) is a difficult time. You may feel more like a dictator than a leader during this time, but these are the years when children learn very necessary skills; like don't touch a hot stove.

This is also the time when a child might start to exhibit both extrovert and introvert tendencies. Prior generations tended to discourage introverted skills like playing alone and encourage extroverted skills like going out and playing with other kids.

\ \ \

Todd lived down a dead-end street in a quiet neighborhood. The parents in this neighborhood all got their parenting letters about the same time, and there were over a dozen children, all born within 2 years of each other.

The neighborhood looked like it was created with children in mind. Norman Rockwell could not have painted a better picture. It was a small road that ended in not one, but two cul-de-sacs after Y-ing off.

There was an open lot a couple of blocks away where a bike track had been created. Close by were two big gullies to play in. There were trees over 60 feet tall to climb as well as wheat fields and apple orchards to explore (not to mention the barns).

But there were always other kids at the bike track. The gullies were the default zone for play wars, and the apple orchards were full of kids during lunch time.

Todd was an introvert and, despite all the room in the area, it was difficult to find time alone. However, on sunny summer days, his mother always told him "go play with the other kids," and would shoo him out of the house.

Todd's mother was an introvert, but she had been taught to pretend to be an extrovert. That was what "normal" people did back then. And, being what she thought was a good mother; she wanted to teach Todd the same thing.

One day Todd found a dirt pile about four feet high in a neighbor's side yard. He spent weeks creating a Hot Wheels track out of the dirt, and he spent hours playing alone in that dirt pile. And he never told anyone, not even the people who owned the house, that he was there. Todd knew, deep down, that he needed a place of solitude that he could go to.

\ \ \

You have the opportunity to help your child learn about themselves and embrace both their extrovert and introvert side. Better yet, you have the opportunity to help them understand more about the basic personalities of extroverts and introverts.

But don't label them at this point. Don't secretly hope that your child is an introvert and subtly push them to introverted tasks. Give them the freedom to explore both.

One skill you can instill in your children is reading. "Teaching young children to read helps them develop their language skills. It also helps them learn to listen."[1] Listening is a skill that almost every person of every age can cultivate more.

The extroverted child

Jeffery showed signs of being an extrovert by age 5. He loved playing with other kids for hours on end and was always talking to them about something. When at home he would walk around the house and say things like: "I'm looking for my ball. Where's my ball? Where's my toy?" But he wasn't talking to anyone in particular, he was just voicing his thoughts.

Extroverted children tend to think out loud. They will talk about what they are doing and what they are not doing. They don't like being alone, and will go throughout the house looking for everyone else just to see what's going on.

But even extroverted children can show introversion at times. Jeffery's 6th birthday party was a smashing hit. There were over 20 other children there and the chaos was an extroverts dream. But suddenly, in the middle of opening his gifts, Jeffery had a fit. Another child had grabbed a toy and was playing with it. Jeffery had a meltdown and started screaming.

Extroverts get over-stimulated sometimes also. Jeffery needed a break, but his parents didn't catch on right away. Instead, they acted like normal parents. They told Jeffery it was okay to share (I don't know why we teach our kids this; adults don't share their toys). Then they started scolding him for his behavior. Finally they gave him a timeout, which is what he needed. After 30 minutes he came out of his room and was his normal, extroverted self again.

Extroverted children need people to talk to, which can be difficult for an introverted parent. Encourage your child to make friends with other kids their age so they have other avenues of conversation, but keep an eye on those friends as well.

Children like to explore their boundaries as they grow up, and finding a friend that doesn't play by the rules can be exciting. Take the opportunity to talk to your child about the real definition of friends.

Another avenue may be to introduce your child to a trusted extroverted family member. It would give your child a person to talk to and you can feel more comfortable about the conversations.

Extroverted children generally need more attention than introverted children. This is not a disadvantage or failing on their part, it's just a fact of life. They need your appreciation and approval. Let them know you are proud of them. Forget the participation awards if they lost a game, but praise them for good plays they made.

They quite often think of nobody but themselves (a habit introverted children share). Teach them about introverts so they understand where you are coming from. Be honest and up front about your need for solitude and let them know that it does not mean you don't love them. Help them be a part of the process and create a schedule that gives them extrovert time and gives you introvert time.

Leading school-age introvert children

I'm pretty sure my mother was an introvert and my father was an extrovert. They both passed away before I began to understand the differences between the two; but looking back, I can see that my father was much more social than my mother.

That being said, my parents pushed me to do extroverted activities. I played soccer, baseball, and football. I was pushed out of the house to "go play with friends." In fact, I cannot think of any introverted activities that my parents encouraged me to do.

I do not blame them. My mother may have been an introvert, but she was raised that introverted traits were not good. It makes sense that she would teach her children the same. And I hate to admit it, but I did the same thing with my kids sometimes.

I played a lot of board games with my kids, but I also took them to crowded playgrounds and encouraged them to "go play with friends."

What I did not do as well as I could have is realize that what gave them the most joy were introverted activities. They liked chess, hiking, bike riding and playing with *Legos* (luckily I did also). They didn't like going to indoor playgrounds in the winter, but I took them anyway. They didn't like group activities, but we did them anyway.

Yes, children do need to experience all that life has to offer, but how much is too much? And how much is too little?

As an introverted parent, are you holding back an extroverted child? Would they rather be playing with friends than reading a book with you?

Are you pushing an introverted child to do extroverted activities because that is how you were raised or because that is what the school wants? Schools don't encourage introversion. "Extra-Curricular activities" is basically socializing after school; like we didn't get enough in school. Dances. Football, basketball, soccer, capture the flag. . . I could go on. Yes, there are other activities like chess club, but those are far fewer than group activities in school.

I remember high school. Chaos reigned, until the teacher arrived. Now that I am older, I actually feel sorry for extroverts. Time between classes and lunch time are the domain of the extrovert; and then there is class time.

You may think that class time is the domain of the introvert with teachers (politely) saying "Sit down and shut up," but that is not necessarily the case. Introverted children have other people all around them so, even though it is quiet; there is a level of constant stress throughout the room for them. Personal space is more of an issue for introverts.

Despite that, extroverts may have it worse in school. Personally, I've never known an extrovert to not talk at all for an hour. That must have been difficult for them. It is no wonder that introverts generally have better grades than extroverts.[2] But being quiet was for the benefit of the teacher, not the introverts. The only real refuge for the introvert in school was the library, which I went to as often as possible.

So, if you are an introverted parent, think back on your school days. What can you do, as a leader in your family, to help your child? First, is your child an introvert or an extrovert?

Talk to your child. Or better, listen to them. Find out what they do and don't like about school. And how do you plan their day after they get out of school? Do you have chores, homework, and dinner (another social event) all lined up for them?

Introverted children need alone time to recharge as much as you do. Why not give them an hour after school to do what they want before homework, etc.? Remember: Leaders listen. What can you do to help your child have a more successful future?

It may frustrate you that all your child does is play video games, but keep in mind that they just spent an entire day being social at school just like you spent an entire day being social at work. Help them to understand what it means to be an introvert and devise a plan that will guide them.

Give them 30-60 minutes after school to calm down before requiring chores and homework. Or find an incentive for getting the homework and housework done. Tell them they can relax, but no phone or computer/game until work is done. However, after the work is done they can play for X amount of time.

Leading your children will not be easy, especially as they enter their teenage years. All you can really do is try to instill good moral values and hope they will follow them. But as they get older and start to spread their wings, you have to let them go and start experiencing the world for themselves. Good leadership is also knowing when to let go.

Chapter 7 ~ Tips to Improve Leadership Skills

Read

"You will be the same person you are today in five years but for two things: the people you meet and the books you read" - Charlie Jones.

"Outside of a dog a book is man's best friend. Inside a dog it's too dark to read" -Groucho Marx

Some of the most successful people in the world are also the most voracious readers. Brian Tracy reads around 50 books per year. Luckily, God created introverts to be natural readers. Not that extroverts don't like to read, it's just not as common to see an extrovert at a coffee shop reading as it would be to see an introvert doing that task.

What's important to remember, however, is that not all reading is the same. Reading the latest gossip or car enthusiast magazine will not help you unless you write a gossip column or fix cars (be honest). If you want to be a good leader, read leadership books. If you want to be a great plumber, read about plumbing. If you want to be the world's best salesman, read about selling.

It's okay if you don't read a book every week; I don't read that fast either. But read every day. Use your calendar to block out reading time if you have to, but do it. And yes, that might mean missing the favorite episode of your television show, but how is that show going to get you closer to your vision?

And, if you don't like to read, tough. Do you want to be a great leader? You should be reading this book because you want to be a better leader. Congratulations on that step! Keep it up, read more. Watch videos on leadership, there are hundreds (if not thousands) available. Are you still using the "no time" excuse? Listen to podcasts on your way to work or while you work out. Or just turn off the television.

Distraction seems to be a way of life now. There are digital billboards, games on phones, entire seasons of television shows just a click away, and more. The list is almost endless. But that may also be the reason paper books are starting to make a comeback. It is so simple to get distracted from your e-book when you get a message, but you can turn the device off when you are reading a paper book.

So if you are driven to distraction, paper books may be the answer. But commitment to reading depends more on you than on the medium in which you read. You can turn your phone off (or on silent) while you read. You can make sure reminders are turned off on your tablet and email is closed on your computer. No matter how you do it, find time to read more.

Critical reading can raise your intelligence; and putting what you read to practice can raise your wisdom. It develops creativity; it helps your career prospects, and much more.

Take notes

Did you catch that above? Not just reading, *critical reading* can raise your intelligence. Highlight items that catch your attention. Put bookmarks on pages that you want to go back to later and read again. And take lots of notes.

Each person has a book inside them waiting to come out, and I encourage you to write a book (even if you do not want it published). But it will never happen without notes. For every book you write on a subject, you should read 50-100; and take notes on what you did and didn't like about each book.

Notes are wonderful and full of imagination. I know a guy named Jeff who carries a notebook with him all the time. He takes notes at networking meetings, church, and even lunch meetings.

I asked to look at his notes once and was surprised when he immediately handed the notebook over to me. The first page had a date of almost two years earlier. There weren't notes for every day and some days had longer notes than others, but the 300-page notebook was almost full.

Jeff doesn't just take notes though; he goes back and re-reads them occasionally. He said he sometimes stumps himself. He will look at a cryptic note he wrote and admit that he has no recollection of what it meant. But most notes are easier to understand. Jeff told me the notebook he was carrying had two one-million dollar ideas in it, and I believe him. He is a multi-millionaire and a consummate entrepreneur.

Have you ever had an idea and thought that it could be worth a lot of money, but done nothing about it? And then, six months later you see someone selling *your* idea on TV or at the store?

What if you had written that idea down in a notebook then sat down and worked out how to make it a reality? It could have been your product on those store shelves. What if you wrote down 1,000 ideas and one of them makes you a million dollars? Would it be worth it?

Journal

Journaling, like note-taking, can be worthwhile or a waste of time depending upon what you do with the information. But there is one big difference between note-taking and journaling: Note-taking is creating written reminders of things you would like to go back over at another time. Journaling is more about reviewing what you did in the past and what you would like to do in the future.

And it is up to you whether you would like to journal and take notes in the same book/document or a different one.

Journaling is like a diary. Each day, couple of days or each week you write down what you did or thought during that time. It is a safe place to document what went on, interactions with other people and thoughts you have about the past and future.

Author Peggy Nolan wrote the article 26 Reasons Why I Keep a Journal (And Why You Should Too) in *Huffington Post.*[1] Here are just a few:

- For accountability
- It's a safe place for all my innermost desires

- I can yell in my journal and no one will hear me raise my voice
- It increases my self-awareness
- It reduces stress

Effective Communication

Okay, we introverts suck at communication. It is awkward and the words never seem to find the correct path out of our mouths so they sound half-way intelligent. But guess what? Extroverts suck at communication also.

Have you ever had a conversation with a person who does nothing but small talk? That person may have something to say, but they don't know how to say it. So by the time they stop blathering and get to the point everyone else has gone to lunch.

We are all in the same boat when it comes to communication.

Learning how to communicate effectively is so important that I think it will put you above 90% of the world in social, relationship, and business aspects. And it is possible that you might be able to teach yourself how to communicate better. But this is one instance where I think introverts could use outside help.

You could look into taking a speech class or a course on effective writing. However, my personal recommendation for every introvert would be Toastmasters. Hopefully there is one near you, because you can learn a lot from them.

And, before you shake your head even more, keep in mind that a majority of public speakers are introverts. I've talked about this a bit in other areas of the book, but remember; when you are on stage you can speak from a prepared script. You do not have to ad-lib or engage in conversation. You speak your peace, and then you leave. What better way can an introvert go into a social situation and leave the star?

The best tip I can give you about effective communication is the same whether you are an extrovert or an introvert: You have two ears and one mouth, use accordingly. That saying may seem to apply to extroverts, but when was the last time someone said something that you didn't hear because you were busy thinking of something else? Practice active listening.

Know Your Weaknesses

What are your strengths? What could you be doing better? Are you a numbers person, or a person who couldn't count correctly with a calculator in hand? Do you have trouble drawing recognizable stick figures or could you create a painting that Monet would be jealous of?

It is important to know your weaknesses, but maybe not for the reasons you may expect. There are some teachers that will rate your strengths and weaknesses; then they will have you figure out ways to raise your weaknesses.

For instance, maybe (on a scale of 1-10) you rate a 6 in leadership, but only a 2 in empathy. Some may give you tips on how to be more empathetic, and empathy can be important. But I recommend working more on your strengths. You could try hard and raise your empathy rating to a 4 or 5, but empathy is not your strong suit.

It's fantastic if empathy is a strength you have, we need more of that in the world. However, if your empathy rating is low, I think it would be better to take that time and effort to raise your leadership skills from a 6 to a 7 or 8. Remember, you are a leader; get a person onto your team who is amazing with empathy and leave that skill to them.

Delegating your weaknesses shows your leadership ability. That doesn't mean you should not work on empathy, it just means it should not be on the top of your priority list.

What are your weaknesses? Try taking some personality tests if you do not know. I talked about the Meyers-Briggs personality type indicator in the Team Building section of Chapter 5. That is a good option. You could also try out my Path of Life Assessment in Appendix 5. You will find that your personal strengths and weaknesses generally mirror how your life is going in different areas.

Practice "The Trick"

Leaders must attend meetings. In person. With other people. And talk. Yes, even introvert leaders. Sometimes those meetings are an excuse to socialize. And sometimes leaders need to attend social events (what I call events designed to talk without a purpose).

Imagine the last several social gatherings in which you attended. How long were you there before you got "that" feeling? You know what I'm talking about. You've said all five small talk items you know (weather, family, weather, great party, and weather) to the three people that you've talked to and now you've run out of little things to say. Your chest is starting to tighten, you've stuck yourself in a corner or a couch and pretended to either listen to the music or watch the sports event on television; and it's time to go.

At this point you are either looking for your significant other to give them the sign (that they will promptly ignore or say *the party's just starting!* if they are an extrovert) or you are deciding which of the twenty-odd excuses you are going to use to leave (one of the reasons I like having dogs).

I can usually last for 1-2 hours at a social event, depending on the company. If this is a social event where I know nobody, 10 minutes can be an eternity. If my extrovert wife is there, she can get me to last about two hours before I'm jumping out of my skin. Anything more than two hours doing nothing but socializing is too long for me, but that also depends a great deal on what else I was doing that day.

I've noticed that what I eat (meaning, how much junk food I've eaten versus healthy food) can have an effect on how social I feel. I can also enjoy social gatherings longer when it's the only social thing I have done for the day and I have prepared for it.

There are ways to make social events more easy-going. This, my friends, is the trick to being a successful introvert leader: Plan your day.

"But I already plan my day, look at my calendar," an exasperated client said. "I have back to back meetings this day, lunch appointments all week, and everyone I know insists on talking in person."

So I will re-phrase it: Plan Strategic Solitude. Does your day sound like the example above? Do you go home every night exhausted and craving alone time?

Introverts are more productive when they have some quiet time during the day. Start planning for strategic solitude by scheduling meetings with yourself and put them in your calendar. Do you have a lunch networking event? Schedule a meeting with yourself for 30 minutes right before that to recharge a bit.

Do you have staff meetings first thing every morning? Put your personal meeting on your calendar right after it. Better yet, wake up earlier so you can have quiet time at home before you go to work.

For every social engagement, schedule a bit of time, even 15 minutes if you have to, before or after to recharge. Do busy work tasks during this time: Clean your desk, reply to emails; whatever it is you do to lower the tension of socializing.

Sometimes even 15 minutes is not possible. Maybe you have a day full of appointments without a break and then you will be going home to a wife and kids. Be honest with your wife; let her know what's going on. But be helpful also. Ask her if you can have an hour alone (after you hug her and see how the kid's days went) so you can recharge. Or, muster your strength and offer her an hour break first; especially if she has had a tough day.

However you do it, find a way to schedule some recharge time in your life. You will begin to unravel if you do not, especially if you have an extroverted job like sales. You may even find that you are better at your job after some recharging time.

Embracing Conflict

> *The better you are at handling conflict the more money you will make. The main purpose of management is to handle conflict. Company CEO's are experts at handling conflict.*

A world without conflict would be all roses, rainbows, and happy people enjoying life; but that is not our world. I have never met a person who didn't experience some sort of conflict in their lives, and conflict is a normal daily occurrence for most people.

Don't think so? How did you feel when you got up? How was your drive to work? Can you honestly say that every minute of this day is being spent *exactly* how you wanted to spend it?

Or did you have a normal day? Did you wake up earlier than you wanted, went to a job that you don't really like, did things that made no sense to you, stayed at work too late, listened to extroverts talk about a whole lot of nothing as if they had nothing better to do with their day, then come home to spouse/kids/no food {insert more here}.

We need our jobs to make money. And I know you love your spouse and kids even when they get on your nerves, but that is all conflict. Even if you take out all the external factors, there is still constant conflict in your mind.

Will 5 more minutes of sleep make me late for work, or will I go to work tired and cranky? Conflict. Will X person overwhelm me with his/her talking as soon as I step in the office? Conflict. How am I going to make money today when I have no clients? Conflict.

But not all conflict is bad. In fact, most conflict is neither good nor bad; it is usually just acting out on two opposing viewpoints of the same issue. For instance:

Current reality: I have some money.

Conflict: I want a new computer.

Acting out: I go to a store to negotiate purchasing a new computer.

Compromise: I trade my money for a new computer.

Peaceful resolution: My receipt is the contract we agreed to.

Successful conflict resolution is when neither party is happy, but both parties are satisfied with the outcome.

Conflict will always be here. The best you can do is to learn how to properly manage it.

Conflict can be caused by many things, the most common of which are belief systems and rights. For instance:

\` \` \`

John and Betty got married. John believed that a wife's job was to keep the house clean and cook, whether she worked or not. Betty believed that a husband's job was to pay all the bills and shower her with gifts, whether she worked or not.

John and Betty have two different belief systems about marriage. How long do you think their marriage will last? It depends on two things: How they talked about their beliefs before they got married and how much they are willing to compromise now.

\ \ \

Belief systems and rights are very similar to each other. We can even take the example above and change the beliefs to rights.

\ \ \

John feels he has the right to come home after a long day of work to a clean house so he can relax and watch TV while Betty cooks dinner. Betty believes she has the right to do what she wants with John's money even if she also makes her own money.

\ \ \

Conflict resolution is about compromise, whether it is in a marriage or the workplace. But conflict resolution requires at least one person to see the big picture, which can be difficult in overwhelming situations.

> *How we see conflict is a test of our leadership.*

How we react to conflict is a testimony of our leadership.

Let me get the worst out in the open right away: Conflict could easily escalate into a full-blown argument when you feel overwhelmed or irritable. It is important to find a nice quiet place to recharge before engaging in conflicting situations.

Feelings of being overwhelmed come from a place of stress, and you need to let that stress go. Even if you can only get away by saying you have to go to the restroom, it will give you five minutes to recharge and regroup. Take those five minutes and use that time to reframe.

Do you tend to have negative thoughts when you recharge? It's time to change that. Negative thoughts interrupt the recharging cycle, so start to reframe the thoughts you have.

If you are in a difficult meeting that is full of conflict, politely excuse yourself to go to the bathroom. Take that time to imagine the rest of the meeting going great. Imagine everyone starting to get along. If you are dealing with one difficult person, sit right next to them when you come back, if you can; it's more difficult for them to be negative about you when they are right next to you.

And find something to agree upon the next time they say something. If nothing else, tell them you are glad they spoke their opinion. They will not be expecting the sudden change, and the shock could help them to start reframing also.

You have a unique position as the introvert leader of the group. You can call a break if tensions start to rise. Or you can take bravery to a new level and call a reframing session and teach your team members how to reframe negatives into positives themselves.

Positive Conflict Habits

Above all else, be nice, especially when others are not being nice. Some people like to spread anger around like it's a reward, don't give in to them. Being nice and staying calm will help others alleviate stress.

The first thing to think of when a potential conflict arises is: "How can I avoid this," especially if the conflict involves you personally. Where within you is the conflict coming from (remember, conflict takes two)? Did someone else get a raise you deserved? Did another person take credit for what you did? Whatever it was, what can you learn from the experience? Avoid conflicts when you can.

Of course, that is difficult to do when the conflict involves other people and you need to step in to mediate. Then the first step is to listen carefully.

Be sure to listen to what each side is conveying. Don't just listen to what they say; listen to what their words mean. Ask questions that call for detailed answers. Sometimes conflict-mongers will rile up a room just like children that crave attention but don't care if it is positive or negative attention. Asking questions that call for a thought-out answer will de-rail these people; they don't have answers for why they are angry.

But even people with a justifiable complaint can calm down when they need to come up with a detailed answer. It is a positive way to get their attention off the anger and onto a constructive subject.

Study the conflict. How did it come about? Where is each side coming from? Study both sides without judgment. Or bring in a neutral 3rd party if you are not able to stay neutral.

Identify the consequences of not resolving the conflict. Introverts tend to run away from conflict, but that is not the best thing for a leader to do. There may be advantages to not resolving it, but communication between the two parties is still a must.

Act quickly. Most conflicts need to be dealt with right away. The conflict will usually continue to escalate until the two sides of the conflict start talking. You need to get in front of the conflict and let the other parties know you are working to help resolve it. If you are working on the conflict, but don't let the other parties know, things could get worse fast and they may undo everything you are working on.

Define the outcome. Detail the ideal outcome for each side. Try to find major and minor points and work with each side to see what they might concede. They will feel more confident about working with each other as both sides start to enjoy small victories.

However you look at it, leaders are expected to be able to handle conflict. The best leaders expect conflict and work toward peaceful negotiation whether the people in conflict get what they want or not. The solution may mean the leader has to give up power or control over something, but that is okay. True leadership is not about power and control; the leader is able to empower others by giving those things up.

Change

"There is nothing permanent except change" - Heraclitus

Change happens whether we like it or not. The length of your hair and nails changes constantly. Your height and weight are never the same from one minute to the next. The temperature of the room you are in is constantly going up and down. And the attitudes of people around you can also change at an alarming rate.

A common saying is that nobody likes change, but that is not really accurate. People don't like the changes they don't like. I know of few people who hate falling in love, but that is a huge change. Most people like getting a paycheck, but financial situations change on a daily basis depending on how much one spends verses how much they make.

Change is necessary, and leaders are change-agents. However, the way change comes about is different between managers and leaders: Managers enforce change from the top down; leaders enact change from the bottom up. For example:

A CEO of a company may notice that profits are down and think the first thing to do is lay off people (manager thinking). Another CEO will show the employees the issue and ask for input (leader thinking).

But the truth is that you can do nothing to change another person. They may decide to change based on new information, but you cannot make them change. You also can do nothing to change the past.

"You must be the change you wish to see in the world"
- Mahatma Gandhi

Change happens when the pain of staying where you are becomes greater than the pain of moving. Yes, change is difficult, and there is a reason why.

Imagine that you are on one side of a jungle and you need to get to the other side, but all you have is a machete. The obvious decision would be to grab the machete and get to hacking.

But you soon realize it is going to take a lot longer than you first imagined. The jungle is dense and there are sudden drop-offs. The going is slow and exhausting. Then, after a lot of hard work, you break through to the other side.

And the next day you have to go back. But this time it will be a lot easier because you did most of the hard work the day before. Yes, you may have made a crude path the day before, but the path is there. As you go back you can improve on what you did, and it will take less time than the day before. Each day that you go down the path it becomes easier until you have a well-established trail.

Most days after that you don't even need the machete anymore. Then you come up with the idea to put gravel down on the path and you have a walkway. It becomes so easy that you almost forget how difficult that first day was.

But I'm not talking about a jungle; I'm talking about your brain. What I just detailed is what happens in your brain every time you start something new. Our brain is wired with electrical impulses called neural pathways. These pathways can resemble walkways, roads, even 8-lane highways.

Have you ever noticed that, after working at the same place for several years, you can forget the drive to work? You may be sitting at your desk then suddenly look around wondering how you got there. The neural pathways that direct your body on how to drive to work had such an easy path that they didn't need a lot of brain power.

Forget walkways or country roads, they had a highway to go down. Then, one day you need to pick something up on the way to work and you have to concentrate on where you are going again because you got off the neural-highway.

Everything you do is subject to the same learning curve. Look back at the example of the child tying his shows in the Competence section of Chapter 3. We start as an unconscious incompetent and can grow to an unconscious competent in everything we do. And each of those steps involves change.

` ` `

It is interesting how we can be resistant to good change. The book of Exodus in the Bible details how the Hebrew slaves were freed of Egyptian rule. They were slaves. They were freed. As they went through the desert God provided Manna (a sweet nourishing food) for them. In response:

And the people of Israel also began to complain "Oh, for some meat!" they exclaimed. "We remember the fish we used to eat for FREE in Egypt" -Numbers 11 (all caps added)

These people were freed from slavery. They had food and water and were promised a better place to live by God, but their brains were so wired for slavery that they wanted to go back.

\ \ \

Creating new neural pathways when you have been going down an 8-lane highway can be difficult, even if those pathways lead to a much better place.

As I said, leaders are change-agents and a part of leadership is helping those you lead with change. Having a clear mission (edict) and a strategic vision (from chapter 4) can help make change easier.

The Desert Experience

Every leader has a desert experience. This is an experience you don't see on television shows or movies (because it does not have a lot of action). However, the desert experience is fundamentally necessary to the growth of a leader.

Muscles get damaged during a normal weight-lifting workout. And, the more weights you use, the more damage a muscle sustains. Muscles don't start to grow again until an hour or more after a workout.[2] Think about the time between working out and when the muscles start to grow as a desert experience.

The body recognizes that it has sustained damage. It is deciding on the best way to repair and grow the affected areas for maximum recovery. Notice that no actual growth is happing yet, the body is just in its planning stage. But significant, specific growth cannot happen without planning.

Planning, however, is only part of the desert experience. Desert experiences happen between phases of great growth. Growth cannot be constant or burnout will happen. I call this time a desert experience because it's like walking across a desert; the landscape does not change much and you may trudge on and on while it seems like you are getting nowhere.

The desert experience is a time of boredom, when very little happens. At least, it seems like that, but that analogy is not actually accurate.

Think of the last time you experienced great growth in your career or your business. It was exciting, there was a lot going on; it was great fun and great stress at the same time. Then it slowed down. Maybe you didn't want it to, but the momentum started losing speed. All that growth created additional serotonin and oxytocin in your brain, and the slowdown also slowed down production of those chemicals.

Many leaders want sustained growth, but that is not a natural process. All of life is an ebb and flow; a time of growth and a time of reflection. But even reflection has its own kind of growth.

Desert time has plenty of opportunity to look back and determine what worked well and what could have been improved. Everything seems great while there is explosive growth, but that is rarely the case. You need desert time to take an honest look because, let's face it, if everything really was going so great you would not be headed for the desert.

So take a step back and re-assess what happened. Write down what went well, and how your successes can be improved. More importantly, document what didn't do well. How can that be changed or eliminated? Ask yourself how this desert experience started. What caused it? Is it similar to what caused the last desert experience? What processes or procedures need to be put into place to help areas of your business, organization, career, or life work more smoothly?

Celebrate!

Congratulations, you did it (or, at least, I hope you did)! You just took a step toward your next level of leadership. I encourage you to read this book again if you read this straight through without acting on anything. This book is not meant to be academic, it's meant to be action-oriented. So give yourself a good reason to celebrate!

You just accomplished more than what 85% of all people do if you completed the action steps in this book, and it is time to celebrate!

But the celebration is just the beginning. Your journey, if done right, will not end even after you die; it will live on through those you lead.

Afterword

There are many places in this book where I have used the pronoun his, him, he etc. I mean this in no way to be derogatory toward women. Women are just as capable (sometimes more capable) as men at being leaders. As long as they are introverts. Not extroverts. Extroverted women have almost as many issues as extroverted men. Someone needs to write a book to help extroverted leaders. Oh, wait, most every other leadership book on the market is geared toward extroverts already. All that "team building," "team exercises," "team bathroom breaks," etc. What we really need is a book on "How Many Extroverts Does It Take To. . ."

Okay, enough extrovert bashing. Not that they don't deserve it, they have been bashing us for centuries. But really, I have some great friends that also happen to be extroverts and I don't hold it against them. And they are easy to spot, aren't they? They answer texts with a phone call (really?), emails with a phone call, queries with an exuberant "let's have lunch!" Lunch is for eating. And reading.

I'm probably going to get into trouble for those last two paragraphs, but I will see if they let them stay in.

The truth is that extroverts are just as needed as introverts. I don't know why God made us so different, but it does make life fun. So remember to text your extrovert friend and send them a virtual hug. It'll drive them crazy. But they will love it, and you for it.

Appendix 1 ~ Core Values Worksheet

This worksheet is designed to help you figure out what your core values are. The easiest way is to print this out (there is a printable version of this worksheet available at www.leadershipintroverts.com) and have a pen or pencil and a highlighter handy.

Circle every item on the list that you feel is a core value. For now, the important thing is just to concentrate on what you feel are core values to you. You should circle between 10-20 items. More is okay.

Once that is done, pick the first two items on the list that you circled and concentrate or meditate on them. Decide which one of the two is more important.

Example: The first two items circled are Abundance and Accomplishment. Spend a little time and determine which means more to you. Put a check mark next to that item. It's okay if both are of equal importance. Go to the next couple of items and try again.

Once you have 6-10 items left it's time to use the highlighter. The idea is to have 3-5 core values maximum. Narrowing it down to 3 core values is the best way to do it; that really focuses your attention on what is important. However, as many as 5 core values are okay.

Start choosing from this list (you can add your own words if you want):

Abundance
Acceptance
Accomplishment
Accuracy
Acknowledgment
Action
Adaptability
Adventure
Adoration
Affluence
Aggressiveness
Ambition
Appreciation
Attractiveness
Authenticity
Awareness
Balance
Beauty
Belonging
Boldness
Bravery
Capability
Carefulness
Charity
Collaboration
Commitment
Community
Compassion
Comradeship
Confidence
Connectedness
Contribution

Control

Conviction

Creativity

Daring

Determination

Devotion

Diligence

Discipline

Discovery

Discretion

Dreaming

Drive

Duty

Education

Effectiveness

Elegance

Empathy

Empowerment

Enthusiasm

Excellence

Experience

Exploration

Faith

Fame

Fairness

Fearlessness

Fitness

Flexibility

Focus

Free Spirt

Friendship

Generosity

Giving
Gratitude
Growth
Happiness
Harmony
Health
Holiness
Honesty
Humility
Humor
Imagination
Impartiality
Independence
Ingenuity
Innovation
Integrity
Joy
Justice
Kindness
Knowledge
Leadership
Learning
Impact
Love
Loyalty
Making a difference
Meekness
Meticulousness
Nurturing
Obedience
Open-Minded
Optimism

Orderliness

Organization

Originality

Participation

Partnership

Passion

Peacefulness

Perfection

Performance

Personal Power

Persuasiveness

Playfulness

Privacy

Productivity

Professionalism

Prosperity

Realism

Reason

Recognition

Relaxation

Resilience

Resolve

Resourcefulness

Respect

Risk Taking

Romance

Sacrifice

Security

Self-control

Self-expression

Sensitivity

Service

Significance

Simplicity

Solitude

Spirituality

Stability

Strategic

Strength

Success

Teamwork

Thankfulness

Timeliness

Transformation

Trust

Understanding

Unity

Usefulness

Vision

Vitality

Wealth

Winning

Wisdom

Zest

Appendix 2 ~ Sample Mission Statements

Below are mission statements from real companies and organizations. Names have been changed to protect the innocent (or guilty). I have included notes on each mission statement.

Mission Statement #1

"AAA Inc. is a spunky, imaginative food products and service company aimed at offering high-quality, moderately priced, occasionally unusual foods using only natural ingredients. We view ourselves as partners with our customers, our employees, our community and our environment. We aim to become a regionally recognized brand name, capitalizing on the sustained interest in Southwestern and Mexican food. Our goal is moderate growth, annual profitability and maintaining our sense of humor."

I like this mission statement. It's specific enough so people know what they do and what they want to do. It is creative and sparks the imagination.

Mission Statement #2

"At XYZ, we are here to provide a unique environment in which anyone can be comfortable. A diverse place where a lasting, active lifestyle can be built. Our product is a tool, a means to an end; not a brand name or a mold-maker, but a tool that can be used by anyone. In the end, it's all about you. As we evolve and educate ourselves, we will seek to perfect this safe, energetic environment, where everyone feels accepted and respected."

Do you know, after reading this, what this company does? We can guess, but this statement is too vague. I like some of the imagery it evokes, but it should be clearer about what they do.

Mission Statement #3

"Maintaining the vision of the founder, {this school} develops Christ-centered men and women with the values, knowledge, and skills essential to make an impact upon the world.

Through its various programs and services , {this school} seeks to educate men and women who will make important contributions to their workplaces and communities, follow their chosen vocations as callings to glorify God, and fulfill the Great Commission."

This would be a good mission statement, if it ended here. It identifies the organization for what it is and what it wants to do. These two paragraphs, however, are not even a third of the mission statement. It went on with numbered lists, bullet points, and more, and more, and more...

Appendix 3 ~ Sample Vision Statements

Here are vision statements I have found from various companies and organizations. It was difficult to find good examples; most vision statements are just extensions of the mission statement.

Vision Statement #1

"Every young person served by the Department of XYZ will become a valued, productive member of their community and lead a fulfilling life."

This was the first vision statement I found during my search. It should have been the last sentence of their mission statement, which was quite good. As a vision statement, this is not so good. It is not strategic; there is no end date... I could go on. Basically, it has no bite to it.

Vision Statement #2

"To leave a sustainable Earth for future generations."

Well, I finally found a vision statement that talks about the future, but it is still vague. It has no end date, and doesn't have much strategy.

Vision Statement #3

"Our Vision is a world without XYZ disease."

This is a strategic statement. It is missing several elements, but it is compelling.

I wish I could have found more vision statements that are truly strategic. But, President Kennedy's statement was perfect, so maybe we don't need other examples.

Appendix 4 ~ Sample Getaway Checklist

Below is a sample checklist for your getaway. You can also get a .pdf version to print out at www.leadershipintroverts.com.

Here are some items you may want to bring with you on your getaway. The first list is if you are going alone, the second list is an add-on if it will be a team event:

- Laptop computer.
- Backup of important files (flash drive, external hard drive, etc.).
- Extension cord, surge protector, network cabling.
- Pad of paper.
- Extra pens, pencils, colored pencils, chalk (in case you find a nice sidewalk), etc.

- Related books, magazines, etc.
- Healthy food (high carb and high fat foods will not help you think at peak performance).
- Itinerary (check the local are for fun things to do in advance).
- Inspirational music.
- Appropriate clothing and shoes for the destination.
- Cell phone and charger.
- All incidentals (toothbrush, comb, etc.).

Add-ons for teams:

- Separate, good-sized computer monitor with appropriate cables.
- White board and pens.
- Presentation pads and pens.
- Nerf guns (Not! The extroverts won't let anything get done. Of course, us introverts would never resort to such childishness, so only bring one for yourself.)

Appendix 5 ~ Path of Life Assessment

The Path of Life Assessment™ by MyCoach.Life

Find out how smooth your Path of Life is by completing this personal assessment exercise. Answer the statements in each category with how closely it pertains to your life right now. 1 = not all like me now. 10 = describes me exactly. Add the total for each category, and then divide by 10 to get your result. Fill in the appropriate box to see if your path of life is smooth or full of bumps.

Be completely honest, this assessment is only for you. It is designed to show you areas that may need some work, but it starts with personal honesty.

You can download and print out a copy of the Path of Life Assessment™ at www.forusintroverts.com if you do not want to mark up your book. You can also find a sample completed Path of Life Assessment™ there in case you need help.

Work	Money	Home	Growth	Health	Fun	Service	Family
10	10	10	10	10	10	10	10
9	9	9	9	9	9	9	9
8	8	8	8	8	8	8	8
7	7	7	7	7	7	7	7
6	6	6	6	6	6	6	6
5	5	5	5	5	5	5	5
4	4	4	4	4	4	4	4
3	3	3	3	3	3	3	3
2	2	2	2	2	2	2	2
1	1	1	1	1	1	1	1

Write a number between 1 (completely disagree) and 10 (completely agree) for each point below			
Work / Career		Money / Finances	
I love my job		I have plenty of money in savings	
I get along well with my boss		I make as much money as I want	
I get along well with my co-workers		I have the money to buy things I need	
There are ample opportunities for career growth		I have the money to buy things I want	
My core values align with the company's		I manage my finances well	
I see myself working here in five years		I keep written track of my finances	

I am paid what my position is worth		I pay my bills on time	
I am comfortable in my office, cubicle, or space		I have no stress over money	
My work is challenging		My retirement amount is on track	
My work is satisfying		My financial future looks good	
Total this section		Total this section	
Divide by 10 and mark the chart		Divide by 10 and mark the chart	
Home Life		Personal Growth	
I live in a city where I want to live		I know my why and core values and live by them	

I live in a house/apt that I want to live in		I have written my personal edict and am accomplishing my vision	
I have all the amenities I want in my home		I like the path my life is currently on	
I have enough personal space		I continually improve myself through professional education	
I like my neighbors		I read as much as I want	
I like the size of my yard/land		I regularly attend positive motivational seminars	
I like my neighborhood		I watch positive motivation videos	
I am happy with the amount/type of pets		I read good leadership and positive	

I have		motivation books	
I like the weather where I live		I am happy with the amount of personal time I have	
I like my commute from home to work		I am understanding of other people's work on their own growth	
Total this section		Total this section	
Divide by 10 and mark the chart		Divide by 10 and mark the chart	
Health		Fun / Recreation	
I am spiritually healthy		I have as much recreation time as I want	
I am emotionally healthy		I have the money to take the vacations I want	
I do not get upset at other drivers on the		I take the time to de-	

road		stress each day	
I am happy with my weight		I relax and enjoy time alone as much as I want	
I am happy with my diet		I enjoy recreation time with my friends as much as I want	
I have an exercise schedule I stick to		I know what recharges me and I regularly do that	
I think positive thoughts about myself		I regularly schedule recreation time	
I eat healthy foods		My recreation/fun time does not get interrupted	
I take responsibility for my mental wellbeing		My job allows adequate vacation time	
I consistently work to maintain my health		I schedule family rec time (10 if no spouse/children)	

Total this section		Total this section	
Divide by 10 and mark the chart		Divide by 10 and mark the chart	
Service to Others		Family	
I routinely volunteer at worthy organizations		I have the feeling of family in my life (whether or not biological)	
I am happy with my level of donating to charities		I am happy with my relationship with my parents (10 if they have passed)	
I routinely ask fellow employees if they need help		I am happy with my relationship with siblings (10 if no siblings)	
My boss knows I am available for him/her		I am happy with my relationship with my significant other (5 if none)	

I routinely ask my significant other if they need help		I regularly contact family	
I offer to help other family members		I have meaningful conversations with family	
My children can rely on me (10 if no children)		I withhold and hide nothing from my family	
I help my neighbors when needed		I am open to creating deeper relationships with all my family	
I donate old clothing		I am satisfied with my contribution to family	
I donate old appliances		I am satisfied with my role in the family	
Total this section		Total this section	
Divide by 10 and mark the chart		Divide by 10 and mark the chart	
End			

About the Author

"When I was younger I was usually quiet. During times when I talked more, my friends would sometimes good-naturedly point it out, which would put me back in my shell. It took me many years to be comfortable with being an introvert and not thinking that there was something wrong with me.

"This book is the culmination of 20 years of trying to understand myself, trying to understand what an introvert is, and what a leader is. There are too many examples of bad leadership that get plastered over the news, but the truth is that those people are not leaders. Leaders put people first. Managers put numbers first." – Dr. Ty Belknap

Ty Belknap received his Doctorate of Strategic Leadership in Life Coaching June 2017, after 10 years in college. He lives in the Pacific Northwest with his wife, children, and whichever dogs they have currently rescued.

Being a self-described "techy-nerd," Dr. Ty has many web sites. Information on his introvert writing can be found at www.forusintroverts.com.

Many of his videos and past webinars on business and leadership can be found on his Webishops (webinar/workshops) web site: www.webishops.com.

His coaching web site is located at: www.mycoach.life.

Bibliography

Barna, G. ed., *Leaders on Leadership*. Ventura, Regal Books,1997.

Cain, S. Quiet: The Power of Introverts in a World That Can't Stop Talking. New York, Broadway Books, 2012.

Clinton, J. R. *The Making of a Leader*. Colorado Springs, CO, Navpress,1988.

Collins, J. *Good to Great*. New York, Harper Collins, 2001.

Dembling, S. *The Introvert's Way*. New York, Perigree, 2002.

Giglio, L. Goliath Must Fall. Nashville, TN, W Publishing Group, 2017

Helgoe, L. *Introvert Power*. Napierville, Ill, Sourcebooks, 2008.

Helgoe, L. "Revenge of the Nerd." *Psychology Today*. September 2010.

Kouzes, J., Posner, B. *The Leadership Challenge*. San Francisco: Josse Bass, 2007.

Lencioni, P. *The Five Dysfunctions of a Team*. San Francisco, CA: Jossey-Bass, 2002.

Malphurs, A. *Developing a Vision for Ministry*. Grand Rapids, MI, Baker Books, 2001.

Maxwell, J. *Developing The Leader Within You.* Nashville: Thomas Nelson, 1993.

Olsen-Laney, M. *The Introvert Advantage: How To Thrive in an Extrovert World.* New York, Workman, 2002.

Robbins, T. *Money: Master the Game.* New York, Simon & Schuster, 2014.

Index

Notes

Chapter 1

---

[1] There are a few studies that say 30%-35% of Americans are introverts. Helgoe, Laurie. "Revenge of the Nerd." *Psychology Today.* September 2010. https://www.psychologytoday.com/articles/201009/revenge-the-introvert. The author starts this article by *saying* that there are just as many introverts as extroverts.

[2] http://www.hrreporter.com/article/11202-open-concept-offices-disrupt-brainwaves-study/.

[3] This was obtained by performing a search for famous American introverts. The list is surprisingly long, so take heart introverts; you are not alone, even though you like it that way.

[4] Clinton, J. R. *The Making of a Leader.* Colorado Springs, CO: Navpress, 1988, 40.

[5] Kline, N. S., M.D. (1981). The endorphins revisited. *Psychiatric Annals, 11*(4), 27-28,30-31,34-35.

[6] Revelle, W. (1995). Personality processes. *Annual Review of Psychology, 46,* 295.

[7] Jalili, S., & Mall-Amiri, B. (2015). The difference between extrovert and introvert EFL teachers' classroom management. *Theory and Practice in Language Studies, 5*(4), 826-836.

[8] http://www.medicaldaily.com/brain-introvert-compared-extrovert-are-they-really-different-299064

Chapter 2

[1] Extroverts have been saying "why can't you be like..." for so long that introverts feel like we don't belong, and we don't... in their city. There have been studies on how extroverts are happier than introverts, but the studies are on extroverted happiness. Once introverts really start flexing their power, we will have much more accurate studies to show the true numbers.

[2] http://www.baseball-almanac.com/hitting/histrk1.shtml.

[3] https://www.followthegls.com/leadership-lessons/10-habits-mentally-strong-people-travis-bradberry/.

Chapter 3

[1] Maxwell, J. *Developing The Leader Within You* (Nashville: Thomas Nelson, 1993), 1.

[2] Barna, G. ed., *Leaders on Leadership* (Ventura: Regal Books. 1997), 23.

[3] Robbins, T. *Money: Master the Game.* (New York: Simon & Schuster, 2014). Some people had concerns about me using this book, but the research looks to be sound. And, frankly, there are not many business people that openly spoke out about the 2001 incident.

[4] Ibid.

[5] Ibid.

[6] Rowe, W. G. Some Antecedents and Consequences of Ethical Leadership: An Examination Using the Kings of Judah From 931 bc to 586 bc. *Journal of Business Ethics, 123*(4), (2014): 557-572. doi:http://dx.doi.org/10.1007/s10551-013-2010-x.

[7] Willis, S. M. Jim bakker: Miscarriage of justice? *Journal of Church and State, 42*(3), (2000): 595. Retrieved from http://search.proquest.com/docview/230010803?accountid=33215.

[8] https://kindnessblog.com/2014/07/23/father-forgives-the-green-river-killer-for-murdering-his-daughter-amazing-display-of-human-kindness/

[9] https://www.webmd.com/a-to-z-guides/news/20101114/oxytocin-more-than-mere-love-hormone#1. Oxytocin was originally thought to be a chemical that was produced by females during pregnancy to aid in the bonding between mother and child. However, recent studies have shown that oxytocin can be produced in the brain by helping somebody in need. Helping somebody up after they have tripped can produce oxytocin. Researchers have even found that watching somebody help another person can produce oxytocin. That could be one reason why we like "feel good" stories so much.

Chapter 4

[1] http://time.com/4176128/powerball-jackpot-lottery-winners/.

[2] https://www.psychologytoday.com/us/blog/smartwork/201004/vision-and-mission. This is a good article on the reasons for creating vision and mission statements. She also goes into why it is important to make each of them specific and different.

[3] Bonin, P., Gelin, M., & Bugaiska, A. (2014). Animates are better remembered than inanimates: Further evidence from word and picture stimuli. *Memory & Cognition, 42*(3), 370-82.

[4] https://www.huffingtonpost.com/yvonne-kariba/10-reasons-we-fail-to-ach_b_7152688.html.

[5] https://er.jsc.nasa.gov/seh/ricetalk.htm.

[6] Kelly, K. W. (2001, 04). Reluctant astronauts. *Astronomy, 29*, 42-47.

[7] https://www.inc.com/lolly-daskal/7-reasons-the-best-employees-quit-even-when-they-like-their-job.html.

[8] Malphurs, A. *Developing a Vision for Ministry.* Grand Rapids, MI: Baker Books, 2001, 98.

[9] https://www.forbes.com/sites/neilpatel/2015/01/16/90-of-startups-will-fail-heres-what-you-need-to-know-about-the-10/#3ba4c9a36679.

[10] Kouzes, J., Posner, B. *The Leadership Challenge.* San Francisco: Josse Bass, 2007, 188.

Chaper 5

[1] Collins, J. *Good to Great.* New York: Harper Collins, 2001, 41.

[2] https://www.psychologytoday.com/blog/self-promotion-introverts/201008/giant-step-backward-introverts.

[3] Giglio, L. *Goliath Must Fall.* Nashville, TN: W Publishing Group, 2017, 96.

[4] http://www.myersbriggs.org/my-mbti-personality-type/mbti-basics/the-16-mbti-types.htm.

[5] Some of the more popular personality type indicators are the Meyer-Briggs (currently free on the Inernet), DISC© Assessment (There are several different DISC© assessments you can take depending on whether it is for personal, business, ministry, etc.) and IDAK®.

[6] Lencioni, P. *The Five Dysfunctions of a Team.* San Francisco, CA: Jossey-Bass, 2002.

[7] https://en.wikipedia.org/wiki/Desmond_Doss.

[8] Cain, S. Quiet: The Power of Introverts in a World That Can't Stop Talking. New York, Broadway Books, 2012, 265.

Chapter 6

[1] https://www.learn-to-read-prince-george.com/why-is-reading-important.html.

[2] Borg, M. O., & Stranahan, H. A. (2002). Personality type and student performance in upper-level economics courses: The importance of race and gender. *Journal of Economic Education, 33*(1), 3.

Chapter 7

[1] https://www.huffingtonpost.com/peggy-nolan/why-i-keep-a-journal_b_3594722.html.

[2] https://www.livestrong.com/article/406021-when-do-muscles-grow-after-working-out-with-weights/.

Made in the USA
Columbia, SC
28 October 2023

25128502R00159